THE WORLD
THROUGH ONE EYE

THE WORLD THROUGH ONE EYE

MY STORY SURVIVING STROKE

DAVE NATHAN

ISBN: 978-1-4834-8525-6 (sc)
ISBN: 978-1-4834-8524-9 (e)

Lulu Publishing Services rev. date: 5/7/2018

FOREWORD

Welcome to my book, this is my story and observations of when I suffered and survived a life threatening major stroke.

This happened a few years ago in my mid forties, working in a well known major supermarket, when Bang, I was hit by a lightning bolt. I suffered an acute mid-brain Thalamic stroke. I don't smoke, don't do drugs, ok I'll have the odd beer but no more than 99% of the rest of the population and I'm certainly no couch potato, my job's quite active. I suppose you could question my diet or the stress in my life but it was more like that old lottery advert for those old enough to remember it, the big old finger came out of the sky, pointed at me without prejudice and said 'it's you!'

That's the difficult bit, not knowing what caused it, living day to day thinking the next one may be in the post, asking yourself 'what do I avoid? What do I need to do? Please not again!' Truth remarkably is for 1 in 5 strokes there is no definite cause so I'm just part of the 20% club.

The main reason for me writing this was during my recovery I was trying to get answers to questions such as 'I can't do xyz, is this normal? How long does this last?' etc, etc. You ask yourself a lot of questions you can't answer which is very frustrating, VERY! Your best qualities are tested to the full and your confidence in the simplest of things is shot to bits. You feel frustration, anger, fear, dejection back to frustration again all at once. However there's not a lot of information out there to help mainly for two reasons.

Firstly, a lot of people have no recollection of what happened or it may be very hazy for them, especially during stroke or in the early stages of recovery. I remember nearly everything and I mean everything, before, during and after, except of course the eleven hours I was unconscious. That is in Chapter two which has been written entirely by my partner in her own words with no input from me. So some who have no experience of what happened to them to draw on can draw on mine and my partner's. I also have age on my side so perhaps my memories may be clearer, this is in no way knocking the elderly, I hope to get there myself one day.

Secondly, a million different people can have a million different strokes and have a million different outcomes so some ailments may be slightly different or completely new. This is my journey so even though I survived and recovered, this is not a checklist or 'to do 'list. I am not a doctor or medical expert but I have had a stroke and survived so all I can tell you is how I felt and what I did. I have spoken to a number of stroke survivors and the one word we all have in common is frustration. If you, the reader, can identify with a chapter, a paragraph or even a phrase, something that can lift you or take away some frustration that you will feel at some point, then this book has done its job.

On that point, you will hopefully notice when reading I do not name anybody not even myself except on the cover. No it's not due to legalities or to protect the innocent but to make it easier for you, the reader, to put yourself into the situation and adapt your real life struggle to it. Actually I tell I lie, there are two people I name but you'll have to read on to see who they are.

I have written this in my own words exactly how it happened for me. They are my opinions and my thoughts and observations. It is a 100% frank account with no elaboration, so I have tried to be as blunt as I normally am so therefore have used the odd plain Anglo Saxon phrase here and there with the odd swear word dotted around, so please be aware of this and don't get annoyed or offended as that's not what is intended. I wanted this to come as straight as I could get it. I wanted it to be honest and blunt so hopefully other sufferers, those who care for and families of those affected can relate to it far more easily. I didn't want this to sound like a doctor or medical expert. Those who know me will know and understand my turn of phrase anyway and hopefully this book sounds like me. This is my story, events, opinions, observations and thoughts from having the stroke, through my early and ongoing recovery and finishes with my 10km run for the Stroke Association less than three years later.

A stroke is a complete game changer and a lot of people have come up to me and said 'I couldn't have done it! I couldn't have gone through it!' No, given the choice I wouldn't have either and I certainly don't wish it on my worst enemy. Remember though and apply this to whatever you want, even if you're thinking what to have for dinner tonight, 'Things in life are so much easier when you take away the choice.' You just have to keep believing, your patience, strength and positivity and all your best and worst qualities will be tested to the full.

I of course have many people to thank. I'm not going to name them as this will defeat the purpose of the book but you know who you are. My family and friends, the medical specialists and my colleagues at work both when I was off and when I returned. You are the reason I'm still here and able to share this. I have been very careful in this book to call myself a stroke survivor and not a stroke victim.

Love and peace to all xx

YET

The biggest word I ever learnt

CHAPTER ONE

The Night Lightning Struck

So there I was, around 9pm, 29th July 2014. I'd just woken up and was trying to haul myself out of bed to go and start my nightshift. I work for a well known major supermarket, I can't say which one but for those who know the area it's the big one between South Wimbledon and Colliers Wood tube stations. I think their favourite colour is orange?? I'd been there for just over six years, starting on the online delivery team and quickly working my way up to hold a couple of small managerial positions instore and was now part of the night shift team. I'd been on nights for a few weeks and I must admit I was still trying to adjust to the sleep patterns. I think humans are like birds, there's something in our DNA that says we shouldn't be awake when it's dark. The previous day I remember struggling to sleep during the day and ended up going down the pub at around 3pm because I just couldn't get to sleep. I finished work at 7am that morning, it was summer, the kids were on summer holidays and I was stuck in the insomniac's circle where you can't sleep so you worry about not sleeping so you can't sleep. Nevermind I thought, a quick couple of beers and I'll sleep like a top. What a bad idea that was, I think I came back at about 7pm to get up at 9pm and felt proper 'Jack in the Box'. Still I went to work as usual that night and worked like a dog as usual but boy did I sleep the next day.

Anyway back to the fateful night. I set off for work as usual for my 10pm start. I felt absolutely fine, I didn't feel tired, no headaches, no dizziness, no indications of what was to come, just walked down the always busy high street to the tube station to get to work and continue my journey from payday to payday. My job was to run the fresh produce section overnight to turn a decimated, half empty department at closing time 11pm into a bulky, well stocked, fresh and inviting palace by opening time 7am.

Everything was about normal, two of us had about twenty boards of fruit and veg to work through which was pretty standard. They get delivered nightly and wheeled down on the mechanical pump trucks by the warehouse guys. This was going to be hard work, it's pretty physical but we knew what to do and we started crashing through it. I went for my lunch at my usual time, about 3am. I'd made some pate and cole-slaw rolls and I went and bought some doughnuts that had been moved into my line of sight all night at the tills. These big supermarkets know what they're doing. I'm always getting people saying 'Bloody Hell, you keep moving things around!' Yes, there's a reason for that.

Anyway I came back from my lunch hour at 4am and continued to break down and put out the big, high boards of fresh fruit and veg. One particularly ugly looking and tall board was right in front of me. 'Which fucking prick stacked this?' I exclaimed rather loudly as some bright spark at the depot had stacked the heavy crates of loose carrots on top of the soft mangoes, at least they used to be mangoes, most were now resembling a messy smoothie. I moved the whole board over to where the carrots went and started to pull the crates of carrots off the top, there must have been five or six of them around head height. I pulled the first crate down with a grimace similar to a famous fictional boxer and crashed it, sorry, placed it carefully into its gap in the racking. I then went for the second.

Now don't get me wrong, to me, a supermarket crate of carrots isn't heavy, but it's not light either and it's awkward at height. It's a two handed job and you have to give it a fair bit of purchase. I pulled it down and went to put it on top of the first one I had so carefully placed into its gap when Whoooosh, I had the most incredible and intense head rush. The world temporarily went on hold and I couldn't move or see properly, I can only describe it as someone pumping a load of hot water into the back of my head at force with a bicycle pump whilst someone blew a loud dog whistle in my ear. That feeling and that noise will stay with me forever. There was no warning, I didn't have a headache, no feeling sick or dizzy or stumbling around, just Wallop. 'What the fuck, what is that? I'm bang in trouble here, this is bad, I think I've blown a blood vessel in my head!' I went completely stiff. I remember grabbing hold of the racking with both hands, starring at the carrots and saying to myself 'Jesus mate don't go down. If you do you'll never get back up' I knew my colleague was over the other side to my left. I tried to look round but my head and eyes would not move. I could only stare at these bastard carrots. I called for my colleague for help. 'Drag me outside' I managed to say. 'I don't want to die in here, I want to die a free man!' I meant drag me out into the road, surely then a passerby would call an ambulance. He only dragged me out into the warehouse the lazy bastard, but then again I'm not the lightest, I know I couldn't drag me that far.

I didn't feel any pain, or perhaps I did but it wasn't registering. I've told that to others whose family members have passed from stroke that they would have felt no pain which gives them a bit of comfort. Nor did I feel the side of my face drop or feel my left side weaken, if it did it didn't register either. Neither did I feel nervous. I've been asthmatic all my life so have been in situations where I've struggled for breath and felt in trouble on loads of occasions, even landing up in hospital a few years before when my lungs decided to pack up, so I felt it was more of a case of what the fuck have I done now? I was also taught Never Fear Nervous. If you feel nervous about something then it means you care about it, like being nervous before an interview or your driving test. In a lesson at school once I remember the teacher saying when you are nervous your body is alert and ready for danger, for example your blood is ready to clot and your senses heighten, so I have grown up never fearing nervous. It's your body's way of telling you I'm ready so bring it on. Your body knows what it's doing so trust it. Nervous is quickly followed by confidence if you remember this. That's why I have always told my friends to stay clear of sedative drugs, listen to your body, you can't be ready and alert on sedative drugs.

I know I went down twice and tried to get up twice by dragging myself by my arms up the racking. This I remember clearly because by this stage my legs had gone, they felt completely disconnected from the rest of me. I heard footsteps nearby so I knew help was close. This is the point at which I became unconscious although I do remember a flash, coming round briefly when the paramedics were there with me. I stood up like a new born foal, feeling the world going round like a spin dryer. I also saw one of my work colleagues at this point who had stayed with me trying to help me stay conscious. 'I'm not going to hospital!' I slurred adamantly to the paramedic who was trying to save my life.

'You're going wherever we take you!' was the reply and out I went again, falling backwards, arms out as if on a crucifix into a stack of bananas.

I don't remember this part completely, just visions and flashes, but apparently I'd already given my phone to my work colleague who had stayed with me. Somehow I'd unlocked it and told them to ring my partner and let them know I was ill, but don't ring my Dad. I ridiculously thought he would give me a bollocking. He had work in the morning and didn't want to wake him up. I didn't work out that my partner needed to do the same so I said the number is under Lemon drops. It isn't?? Who the fuck is Lemon drops? I don't call anyone Lemon drops, honestly. I probably haven't eaten Lemon drops since I was at school. There's absolutely no relevance in me saying that but by this time my brain, as you can tell hopefully, had stopped making any sense and was trying to shut itself and my body down and I was running on empty as they say. I've been told I was taken down to the ambulance in our delivery yard by scissor lift strapped in to some sort of upright stretcher with an oxygen mask on. It must have looked similar to that scene from Silence of the Lambs. The small amount of life I still had in me was now in the lap of the Gods, or more accurately, in the lap of the paramedics taking me to hospital.

CHAPTER TWO

Behind The Curtain

Written entirely by 'Lemon Drops??'

The phone rang too early in the morning....I chose to call ignore the first call. It's obviously an idiot calling at this time......no, it could be my partner, my sister, somebody who needs me. Managing to shake off my slumber, I answered, hoping it was a prank call, not bad news. One of my partner's colleagues was speaking quite calmly though hurriedly.

"What?!? Is he breathing?" I asked. "It must be an asthma attack. He shouldn't be passing out, just like that. I'm coming with his pump." The conversation was quick and informative. There was no time for pleasantries. Then I heard him say "Is that my babe? Tell her not to phone my Dad. I'm not going to hospital...." I told him that he bloody is and that I'll see him there. I couldn't hear him anymore...

"Pinch him, slap him. Don't let him go. Keep him awake! Please. I'm letting you slap his face, do anything, do it!!!" I remained on the phone, listening whilst sheer panic ran through my veins. Within seconds, the ambulance arrived and gave instructions on where they were taking him. I was already half dressed. The fifteen minute walk to the hospital became a seven minute sprint.

At A&E, I was greeted by an Irish nurse who initially tried to calm me down as I fired her with information. She brought me to a room near the Trauma department and left me there for a while. It seemed like an eternity. Finally she returned to verify my details, my partner's Dad's details and scuttled off again. It was too long before she broke news of what was happening now and whether I could see the love of my life then she warned me that he wasn't awake and remained unresponsive. I understood what she said though couldn't fathom why. I felt my innards collapse though reminded myself that I need to be strong. "I need to be with him. I need to see him, he's on his own like this."

The nurse ushered me through to a ward where doctors were too busy to notice that I stood there. I was desperate and tempted to pull open every curtain until I found him then was approached by a nurse. She led me to him. He lay there, calm though not relaxed. I immediately kissed him, believing that I could wake him up...his hand moved. A doctor walked in, verified my identity and explained what had happened. They had already carried out numerous tests. While she spoke, I listened but only picked bits of information from what she said. She mentioned blood clot on the brain, the need for medication to save him though it could be fatal. I said yes but retracted it as soon as it flew out of my mouth because I thought his Dad might want to know about the procedure first. I had to remember that I'm not the only one who loves him. His Dad was on his way. It was a waiting game. Within minutes his Dad arrived, listened to the same diagnosis and treatment the doctor told me and answered immediately, "Give it to him. I don't want to see him like this." He signed the document for the drug to be administered. His Dad and I watched closely as the nurse did.

This is the moment where you want instant results, for my partner to just open his eyes and come on home now! He didn't. The nurse asked us to leave as they had to take another scan of my partner's brain to see if the blood thinner administered had eased his blood clotting further on his brain. Realisation hit. I felt weak. My partner has just had a stroke! He's not a smoker, heavy drinker or have high cholesterol. Why him? I needed air to try and think straight. How could this happen? Had I done something wrong? Could I have prevented it? Possibly not, my partner is rather stubborn and stuck in his ways. I feel helpless and uncontrollably cry for a short time before realising my partner needs me now more than ever.

After getting two minutes of air, both his Dad and I share a short cuddle before being shown in to see him again. Both of us continue to talk to my partner, who I'm convinced now is just sleeping. I was adamant that he'd soon wake up and start sharing his bad jokes, which were annoying before but at that moment, I loved. Doctors informed us of my partner's status, which at this point was stable and admitted him to the acute stroke unit. I had reached another state of shock, denial. They can say what they want but my man is coming home with me, fit as a fiddle. No matter how long it takes. They gave us directions to the ward but I insisted to take him. A porter with the least manners or intelligence had been sent to bring us all there and I couldn't help but let rip on him for his carelessness and rude remarks. This was the only part of the NHS service we received, which let their excellent reputation down.

On the ward, all staff were friendly, understanding and accommodating. I have high regard for the work they do and what they have done for us. We were instructed to wait in the day room for a while, which gives me a little time to plan the rest of our lives together, IF there are any changes. We were shown through to his bed, his Dad offering me the seat first. No thanks, my place is sitting on the bed, whispering in my man's ear. I admit, while his Dad left the room and we were alone behind the curtain, I whispered things that would wake him up, if you know what I mean....sometimes his hand twitched.

"Did you see that?" I asked excitedly to the doctor from the morning shift. Initially, she hadn't been in favour of me sitting on the bed or even whispering in his ear but now she had to agree to my alternative medication. "Keep talking to him, he seems to be responding. I can tell you two are very close." I smiled at her comment, a tear close to my eye. We stayed there, his Dad and me, watching intently while the doctors carried out even more tests. I assisted one of them putting on support stockings, to encourage the blood flow. 'He'd like these.' I giggled to myself, thinking about the kind of remark he'd make if he was awake. It won't be long until he is. The doctors left for at least half an hour before one came back with news.

She said in the most calming manner, that the next 24 hours were crucial. He needs to be alert within this time for things to look promising. I couldn't comprehend what the doctor was saying. They actually believed that he wouldn't come round. You're chatting bullshit! That's what I wanted to tell the doctor, raw, just like that, though I refrained, remembering that I was the presence of my future father-in-law. What showed on my face was disbelief.

"No, he's alright. You don't know him like I do, he just needs some rest."

"I don't think that you understand, he may not make it. You need to understand-"

"No. You need to understand. You've cut up his clothes so he'll need some fresh ones to come home. At the very least, some slippers!"

It was 7.15a.m when I left for home for those fresh clothes and both the doctor and his Dad thought I had lost the plot. Every hour was excruciating. With every ounce of my being, I wanted my partner to prove them wrong for us both to tell the medical staff that, in my partners words of denial, 'don't know their arse from their elbow'.

1.30pm. Seven hours and thirty minutes since their 24 hour warning and no real change. I still say he's sleeping. His Dad reminds me that I haven't eaten and neither had he. We reluctantly leave, asking the afternoon shift nurse to call me if there's any change. My partner's Dad drops me home, where in the shower, the phone rings. The call I didn't want to miss. After slipping on the suds, I frantically scamper to answer.

A young lady asks for me, I confirm. I don't have any patience, the person the other end of the phone wasn't speaking fast enough. "What is it? Has something happened? Give me five, ten minutes, I'll be there. Tell him I'm on my way." Words couldn't leave my mouth quick enough, unable to speak clearly in the Queen's English, even forgetting my manners. The nurse replies telling that he's woken up and in bed. To be honest, I'd heard enough and just wanted to speak to my love. I wanted to hear him, feel him, be with him. I was anxious and she was informing me on his vitals, I was interested but save that for later.

"Do you want to speak to him?" Finally! "YES!" I held my breath, scared of what emotion would expel first without my control. "Hello babe." He spoke exactly how I remembered. It seemed like it was ages ago since I last heard his voice. Tears of joy and excitement erupted uncontrollably though a huge grin donned my face. "Babe, I love you." I replied. We shared a short intimate few minutes on the phone.

I noticed he spoke with a slur, which he apologised for. I didn't care, my love was awake and I knew they (the doctors) were chatting shit. 24 hours, my arse!

After contacting his Dad, I ran back to the hospital. I was trembling with excitement, with this feeling I could conquer the world with its challenges. It seemed that I was travelling fast though everything had slowed down considerably, even the lift up to the ward couldn't get me there quick enough. I approached his bed.

"Hello babe. You ok?" He asked, as I wandered back slowly. I wanted to embrace him and did so but saw him confused and disorientated in the bed. The following few hours were very emotional. His Dad had returned and we all shared and listened to each other's experiences of the past 12 or so hours. I felt even more protective than ever, more responsible and more in love. My partner had gone through a trauma, a trauma which nobody can explain in the same way. Unfortunately many people don't survive, those in their senior years especially.

Some can call him lucky, doctors put it down to theory, his age, the amount of time between the stroke and medical help. Call it what you will, the experience from the other side is still current. My partner is still recovering and so am I. I've been upgraded without consent, something that I'm proud of as a mother, partner, carer. At least until my partner feels he is strong and confident enough to return to the usual routine. In fact, I'll always be there, as MY usual routine.

A few days later, I arrived early one morning to help him shower, only having two hours sleep myself, but was running on adrenaline. He was asleep but woke when I moved the curtain. "Good morning, babe." In the bathroom, we shared the most intimate embrace ever between two people. I chose to get him in the shower, he used this as an opportunity for some privacy. It wasn't lust, it was real love and appreciation.

Visceral. The fact that we were in the Acute Stoke Unit in St. George's Hospital didn't bear any relevance to what followed. We shared and cared for each other in that bathroom like our lives depended on it.... in a way, it did. On returning to the hospital bed, we all joked about bed baths and nurses, he hadn't lost his sense of humour, which I know he was happy about.

The next few days visiting him in hospital became easier, for both of us. There were more MRI scans, motor skills tests and stringent medication routines. Let's get back to normality, get his brain doing usual things before connections fray. On his discharge, we were elated. In hindsight, I know now that we were both apprehensive on what was to follow. All I knew was, Stroke made us stronger.

CHAPTER THREE

Awake in Hospital

I came round with that weird feeling you get when you wake up in a strange bed, it takes you a few moments to remember where you are. This was different though, this didn't feel like a normal waking up feeling, this was taking ages to work out, where the fuck was I actually? It felt rather dull and dark so I figured wherever I was it must be early morning but I could barely see. Something's not right! For a start I had no peripheral vision, my world had suddenly shrunk by two thirds and the middle bit I could see was a mess of blur and colour. This was very confusing, I tried to focus but my eyes would not obey, I had some serious double and blurry vision. I was aware I had drips in both arms and I could make out other beds. I then realized I was in hospital. 'How long have I been in here?' I wondered to myself. I leant forward but I was stopped by a nurse's hand holding my left shoulder. 'Hello' she said 'Lay back and relax.' I tried to reply but my mouth wouldn't obey either. All that came out was a loud 'URRRRRRGH', where the hell did that noise come from? 'Relax' said the nurse 'You've had a stroke' When I heard that the world stopped.

'URRRRGH' I let out again and I tried to get my head together but I was all over the place, my body just wasn't responding and I couldn't think straight. I couldn't seem to move my arms or legs and my head would not go where I wanted it to. There's something else, something I couldn't quite put my finger on and I also felt something strange on my legs. I had these long pads on them, the sort of things you see a batsman wear in cricket and they were rippling up and down. They were electric and were keeping the blood flowing around my lower half. Stroke, no didn't hear that, no way, I'm too young, can't be that bad, stroke? I admit I felt a bit of panic which was fuelled by overwhelming confusion. I remember immediately jumping to conclusions. OK I thought, now relax, I'm not mentally disabled, I'm sure I'm thinking ok but I can't work this out and physically I feel shot to fuck. It felt like someone had pulled my plug out and I immediately thought this is as good as I'm going to get for the rest of my life. I couldn't move properly, see properly or talk at all. In a rash moment of stupidness, I thought to myself 'I'm not spending my life like this. The missus has her hands full with the children, I can't expect her on top of all that to feed me every mealtime and wipe my arse every five minutes. If I can't grab my bollocks this second then I'll find a way to roll off this bed pulling all these wires out and I'll end it right now'. My right hand slowly made it down to my bollocks and I grabbed them. I looked at the nurse, who was looking back at me holding my bollocks with an inane grin on my face. Fuck knows what she must have thought but I didn't care. I knew right then I had physically achieved something therefore I had something to work on but what is this other thing I can't work out?

I was then given a small teaspoon of water to drink. This was to make sure I could still swallow as it's quite common to lose this ability after a stroke, in fact your whole digestive system can stop. I managed to swallow the small amount of water and I heard a doctor say 'Give him a drink.' In my panic I had totally forgotten I was gasping. As I sipped my water from a cup the nurse was holding for me I was asked my name and where I was. I got my name right but I said I was in St Hellier hospital, I knew this from a conversation I was convinced I had on the way here. I was actually in St Georges in Tooting, about a mile from work where I had the stroke, but no I was adamant I was in St Hellier at Rose Hill. I could not just say words like we all have been doing all our lives. This was now different, it was as if someone had cut the string between my brain and my mouth, those that know me well will know I never have a problem just speaking out but that had gone. I was having to imagine the word spelled out in mid air in front of my eyes and then try to read them out. This was hard work as I was also trying to remember how to spell simple three letter words as I couldn't concentrate. I just couldn't spontaneously speak. For that reason I tried to say as little as possible but I was soon to say the hardest few words I've ever had to say.

Again and again I was asked my name and where I was and again and again I gave my name and said St Georges even though I was convinced I was in St Hellier. I lost count of the amount of times I was asked this but they were making sure I was alert and not slipping back. Remember when I blurted out Lemon drops? Anyway the nurse asked me if I wanted to ring my missus. Yes of course I did, she must be worried as she was probably at this moment getting the kids ready for school so I'll give her a ring to let her know I'm OK. I tried to look around the wall for a clock to check the time but my eyes just would not move and I had the strangest double vision, it was the weirdest sensation. I managed to find the clock by moving my head away to my left and looked at it. I found myself looking at this old hospital issue clock and it just looked straight back at me. I could see the face, the numbers, the hands but I couldn't tell the time. What the fuck is wrong with me? I'm going crazy. I know I can tell the bloody time so why can't I tell the bloody time now? It was then I was hit with the next bombshell. 'Your other half has been up here all day, she was so worried, she's only just gone home.' said the nurse. Hang on I thought and I spelled out in mid air and said out loud 'What's the time?' I heard myself speak it out in a massive slur. 'It's 3.30pm' came the reply and I really struggled to take this in. I couldn't work this out at the time but I had been unconscious and unresponsive for around eleven hours.

The nurse rang the number and I heard her say 'There's someone who wants to talk to you.' I needed to tell my missus I was ok but I also knew I was almost incoherent and I didn't want her hearing me talking like that. I'm a bloke, a rock my missus can rely on. I didn't want her knowing I was ill but I needed to reassure her I was ok. I took the phone and spelled out 'Hi babe'. I then spelled out 'I love you' and with every sinew at maximum I tried to say it without slurring. I failed badly, it must have sounded awful. It was the hardest sentence I've ever had to say but I heard her respond and knew I had reassured her. But what was this other niggling thing I couldn't work out? I put the phone down and I heard my Dad come in and thought he had come to take me home. He sounded worried but knowing my Dad was there now filled me with a bit of confidence, the same way it has always done since I was a kid. Again I was asked my name and where I was. Again I said my name and I'm in St Hellier. ' Why do you think you're in St Hellier?' said my Dad. Then I dropped a bombshell back. Again I had to spell the words out in mid air first so this took a bit of time to get out. 'Mum sent me here 'I said. I couldn't see properly but I could feel my Dad just looking at me. 'The ambulance stopped at St Anthony's. I had a chat with her and she sent me here to St Hellier' I could tell my Dad was still just looking at me not saying a word. My Mum had died 23 years earlier from cancer in St Raphael's hospice next to St Anthony's hospital in Cheam. Now sorry but I don't believe in all that life after death stuff, never have done, never will do. If there is such a thing as reincarnation then knowing my luck I'll come back as me. The only member of my family that I knew believed in reincarnation was a great uncle of mine who literally lost an absolute fortune gambling on the horses. He gambled every day, right up until his death in his late nineties, always trying to beat the bookie, which as we all know is impossible. My grandma always used to say 'You'll never see a bookie in scuffed shoes,' how very true. Before he died he said he was going to come back as a racehorse, a good one in a classic race such as the Derby. When the stalls open, he's going to go straight over to the favourite and kick it straight in the bollocks. Then he'll jump the rail and make a bolt for the bookies enclosure and try and take out as many as he can. If you ever see that happen at a racecourse, it's my great uncle. Anyway all I can tell you is I am convinced I had a conversation with my Mum, to this day I don't know what it was about but all I know is it felt as real as any conversation I've ever had at work, at home, in the pub, anywhere. People keep telling me it was a near death experience but I like to try and believe it was just a vivid dream or my brain playing tricks in a panic, that's much more believable to me. 'No you're in St Georges' said my Dad and I was even more confused because I always trust what he says.

So there I was, confused, frustrated, worried, unable to move properly, no proper vision, numerous drips in the back of each hand, unable to really speak, my legs rippling away, trying to come to terms with what had happened and make sense of it and this other thing I couldn't put my finger on, but alive and aware and my Dad and my missus were now there with me. One thing that definitely was working was my bladder. I'd clearly been pumped full of liquids, medication and fuck knows what else for eleven hours to save my life so I was needing the piss bottle every half hour to get rid of it all or that's what it felt like. I needed help with the bottle, firstly I had no co-ordination and secondly I had drips in each arm restricting my movement further. I was pissing like a pregnant racehorse and for anyone who's ever used one, no matter how much cock you've got in that cardboard bottle it still feels like you're pissing the bed. It was during one of my piss episodes that I worked out what this niggling extra thing was. As the nurse was talking to me and helping the old bellringer into the bottle, I realized that everything she said and did happened moments after she said it. Bingo, that's what it is. It was all out of sync. I didn't know at the time but my stroke was in my mid brain around the Thalamus so certain signals were getting slightly delayed. Imagine a car crash during rush hour on spaghetti junction. The odd vehicle will get in and out and this was now like the signals trying to get in and out of my brain. The experience I was having had just complicated further as it now resembled a badly dubbed movie. I was hearing things then seeing them happen moments later.

This is where all the denial started. It gets you without warning but it's totally natural and it's not all bad. There I was, I was right in the middle of a completely life changing event, but all the time I'm thinking it can't permanently be this bad and you don't believe it. A couple of days in here and I'll be back home. You see your brain is the most amazing piece of kit but it does play tricks on you. Mine had just gone through this huge trauma but it was still telling me I was ok and reminding me of things I knew I used to be able to do, simple everyday things such as going for a piss, moving my arms and legs, etc. This makes you believe you're not as ill as you really are. You only realize this as you recover and realize further down the line how far you've come. You remember what you were like, two, three, six months ago. It also makes you realise how unprepared you are to die. Is the insurance up to date? Will the wife and kids be taken care of? Who's going to pay for the funeral? If you've got dependants and haven't checked for a while, then do it.

I then had to go for a scan, to this day I don't know what it was but they probably told me, I just didn't take it in. They wheeled me out on my bed and I travelled down a couple of floors in the big lift and through a few corridors. I lay there trying to enjoy the journey and just look up and stare at the different ceiling tiles. I had no peripheral vision so it was like the scene out of Trainspotting with him on the stretcher in hospital after OD'ing on heroin playing to the tune Perfect Day. Remember the two sides blacked out as he looks up? Well now imagine a blurred, version of that with double vision and you'll have a rough idea of how it looked for me. We ended up in some medical scanning department. I knew there were a few staff around me and they were talking to someone in another room through a microphone. One of the nurses bent down and said 'I'm just going to give you an injection. This will make you feel as if you've wet yourself.' I don't know what this injection was, some sort of dye I think to make my scan clearer but yes, it really felt like I had pissed myself, it was really odd. Anyway I was told not to move at all and they wheeled me lying on the bed, feeling like I'd pissed myself, into this big metal drum. I think I moved my arm and this voice came out of a speaker 'Try not to move, keep still.'

I heard it but it didn't compute and for some strange reason I couldn't work out how to stay still so I tried to sit up. Again I heard this voice telling me to keep still and again I tried to sit up so I could understand. This happened four or five times, the doctor telling me to keep still must have been pissed, like a parent when their kid does the opposite of what they tell them, but I remember coming out and everyone being really calm. I was so confused, I knew what I had to do but had no idea how to do it! My body and brain somehow felt like long lost strangers, sitting next to each other in silence. They finally gave up and wheeled me back to the ward without having my scan.

I got back to the ward and tried to rest, trying to make sense of what the fuck had happened to me. My Dad and missus were still there and I managed to work out I was the middle bed on one side of a ward of six beds. I was still attached to my various drips with some sort of tap in the backs of both hands that looked like a mini draught beer pump system and I still had my legs rippling. My visitors left later on and I honestly thought that would be the last time I saw them. I was convinced I was going to die in my sleep and this was going to be my last night on Earth but I didn't want them to know that so I said Goodbye as I usually would. I was now on my own and this was going to be the first of many nights where I would be seriously afraid to fall asleep.

I woke the next morning to the sound of cluttering tea trays and busy people on the ward. Medication time. Again it took me a while to work out where I was, again through a blurred mess of colour and I realized I hadn't miraculously got any better in my sleep, but relieved I hadn't died either. I was still attached to various drips and the contraptions on my legs so my movement was limited and my eyes felt like they had been glued into my sockets. However, next came the highlight of the day. The bed bath team came onto the ward and I thought they would go round in order and me being in the middle bed, I thought I'd be second or fourth depending on what way round they went. But no, the bathing trolley parked right next to me, the young nurses whipped my curtain round and I was going to be first. I'd like to think they made a bee line for me because I was obviously a lot younger than the others on my ward. I was fresh meat and they were eager to check out their new patient. The truth is of course they were extremely professional and caring as all nurses are.

I was allowed a bit of light breakfast, which I fought like mad to get to my mouth. My arms were very slow and I still had my drips in but they were starting to listen to me and as far as I know, I didn't spill any food or my essential morning cup of tea, but boy was it a struggle. Afterwards I just lay on my back with all my drips in both arms, on my back, looking up wondering what was in store for me today. I worked out I must have brain damage of some description because my movement was so poor and I could only see the middle third of the world and it looked a real mess. I couldn't move my eyes, I couldn't really move anything, everything noise and vision was out of sync, I couldn't talk properly but because I could work this out, I figured that mentally I wasn't too bad. Wildly confused, yes, disorientated, definitely, but I knew where I was and reckoned I had most of my wits about me. I was still pissing like a broken fire hydrant, they must have filled me to the brim with fluids while I was unconscious but at least I knew that particular system in my body was working. I was very calm but in the back of my mind I knew something very serious had happened to me.

I was woken out of a little snooze by busy doctors around my bed. Medication time. They wanted to do a few checks and then have another go at giving me a scan, the one I should have had last night but couldn't work out how to keep still. It was then I was told what had happened to me, the temperature seemed to drop in the room. I had suffered an acute mid brain thalamic stroke, a pretty nasty one caused by a large blood clot right in the middle of my head. Now you think of a blood clot as a small ball, no bigger than a tiny ball bearing blocking a small vein or artery. I was to see my head scans, taken while I was unconscious, at a later date and it really shook me up. There was a large dark area that covered most of the middle of my head. It was a miracle I was even alive, let alone conscious and moving with my eyes open after two days. The medical staff hadn't really given me much of a chance of any sort of recovery but because I was at work and close to St George's I was treated quite quickly. Your thalamus is a small gland that sits on top of your brain stem and pings information from your brain to parts all over your body which is why I had no or little co-ordination. It also handles your sensory and survival tasks such as sight, sleep patterns, conciousness together with heartbeat, blood pressure and breathing. I knew I was damn lucky, whatever happens from now on, but in true English fashion I hadn't forgotten my manners and I apologized to all the doctors about yesterday's failure at my scan, my speech still sounding like a big drunken slur. Again I felt a hand on my shoulder and a reassuring voice telling me not to worry, you were so dazed and confused they said. I went down and had my scan this time without any problems and was then wheeled down to see the eye specialists. I was sitting in a wheelchair in what I worked out was a packed waiting area, my arse feeling like it was sticking out in the fresh air, out of the always too short hospital gown, when I saw a blurred darkly dressed figure in front of me asking questions to what I presume were the doctors. I didn't realize who it was because of my poor sight until she opened her mouth and spoke to me, it was my missus. I hadn't recognized her.

I didn't wait long before I was wheeled in to see one of the specialists who did a few tests and told me what they thought. One of the first things they told me was because of what happened my eyes had a difference of fourteen, whatever that is, and would take around eighteen months to recover. Did I hear that correctly? Eighteen months? Part of me thought 'Fuck that's a long time, this must be really bad because I've never been ill for that long?' The other more dominant voice in my head thought 'Bollocks, it can't be that long. I'll be back at work by Christmas.' Denial! Anyway I went through some really challenging sight tests and my eyes felt like they were glued at different angles into the back of my eye sockets. I just couldn't seem to look at and focus on anything they told me to. It felt like all I needed was for someone to whack the back of my head with a plank and that would release whatever was holding my eyes and they would reset like the reels on a fruit machine. There must be an easy way of doing this, something simple I'm not doing. Both eyes were really starting to hurt like a tired achy hurt because I was trying so hard to focus on anything, but then came a moment of clarity. The specialist covered one eye for a different kind of test and I could see clearly. My stroke had weirdly unsynchronized my eyes but I could still see out of both of them like a damn chameleon. Because of this I'd also lost all depth perception. I was seeing two images at two different angles that moved across each other hence the double vision but if I shut one then I could see just the one image. This didn't help the fact that I had no peripheral vision or that I had no depth perception but it gave me a starting point. I could now see things but couldn't tell where they were, if they were right next to me or twenty feet away. My life now went completely Wayne's World, remember the 'Camera One, Camera Two, Camera One, Camera Two' scene? I did this constantly, left right, left right, to try and get rid of the blurry, double world I was stuck in. It did work to a point but boy did I give me the most intense, hangover style headache so wherever possible I just tried to keep my eyes shut and relax. I was then wheeled to a different part of the department where a large, Asian man with a big, long beard spoke with me. He told me I would do most of my recovering in the first three months, after that natural recovery slows but there are other options such as surgery. I heard that bit loud and clear and I politely declined. In my own head I was screaming 'No way surgery, no fucking way. You're not operating on my eyes or my brain!!'

I felt myself being wheeled back in the ward and wanted to see who I was in there with so I shut one eye and had a look around. Now I could make out the six beds, the windows, the layout and who was in there with me. I was the youngest by at least twenty years which made me think, stroke? Surely I'm too young? Clearly not. Opposite me in the middle was a sweet, elderly man who kept repeating the same things over and over again. Normally this would really piss me off but this was the beginning of a new patient and sympathetic me and I knew the guy had been through something similar and was equally confused. The same applied to the poor bloke opposite me to the left. He kept suddenly shouting out, declaring he'd been burgled and needed to phone the police. Again the guy was so confused he had no idea really where he was or what was happening. Either side of me were two quiet fellas that spent most of their time asleep. The one that affected me the most was the poor old guy opposite me to the right. He never regained consciousness the whole time I was in hospital, his elderly sister sat with him hour after hour waiting for a miracle, a slight movement or change in condition, anything. We were all hoping with her. That could have and perhaps should have been me. Was it just sheer luck? I was at work and was noticed quickly, this poor bastard could have been on his own at home. To this day I sincerely hope they have all recovered to some extent and are back home with their families.

I now wanted to know what caused it. Why the fuck at my age have I had a stroke? I'm too young, I don't smoke, don't do drugs, ok I'll have the odd beer but no more than 99% of the rest of the population and I'm certainly no couch potato and my job's quite active. I suppose you could question my diet or the fact that I support Arsenal and they like to put me through the ringer every week but incredibly one in five strokes never have a definitive cause and I was one of them. I was part of the 20%. It was more like that old lottery advert for those old enough to remember it, the big old finger came out of the sky, pointed at me without prejudice and said 'it's you!' That for me is both the difficult bit and the easy bit. I used to lie there thinking about the difficult bit, what caused it? What do I need to stay away from? What do I need to avoid? This changed into the easy bit, I've got nothing specific to avoid or fear therefore just be sensible.

I was asked every couple of hours or so and at every medication time by the nurses for my first few days if I'd had a bowel movement which I hadn't. This was to see if my digestive system was back up and running. On day three it happened. I felt the urge and called for the nurse who brought me a bedpan. No sorry, I want to get up and use the toilet like I've been doing for the past forty odd years. The problem was I hadn't walked a single step since being admitted to hospital and this could prove too much for my limited co-ordination and seriously weak body, still I wanted to try. This would require permission from a doctor and a physio, two people's consent for me to get up and take a shit! Do I need to put my hand up and wait to be excused as well? The professionals were amazed I was even awake, let alone wanting to take a walk. The doctor came over, asked me a few questions and saw I was very determined. His point was I shouldn't be walking, it's far too soon. My point was I wanted to go to the toilet in a more recognized, civilized fashion. The doctor agreed so it was now down to the physio. I had to push against her first with my left arm, then with my right. 'He's got left sided weakness' she told the doctor. 'No, I'm right handed' I replied. 'Try my legs!' I then had to push against her again first with my right leg followed by my left. 'Your right side is weaker' she said. 'No' I said again, 'I'm left footed.' When I was younger I was extremely left footed at football, it was much stronger than my right leg, my chocolate leg which was only there to make up a pair. My first hero when I was a kid was a left footed Arsenal player, the cover of this book is the clue to his identity. The physio looked at me and agreed I could walk to the toilet. Off came the rippling pads and out came the mobile wheels for the drips, I felt free of the bed, now how would I manage this? The physio stayed with me as I swung my legs off the bed very slowly and began to sit up. This felt really weird, a strange little head rush but I wasn't stopping now and I certainly wasn't waiting for the physio to change their mind. I shut one eye and very slowly and with great concentration planted my feet into my brand new slippers and with a little wobble I stood up. It felt great to be up but at the same time I felt like I was on a boat and the room started to spin and twist. I could see the toilet door with one eye, right at the entrance to the ward, no more than thirty paces away and with the physio's assistance, I took a very slow walk one step at a time towards the toilet door.

It felt like it took a good fifteen minutes to reach the door, I had to think about picking my leg up, moving my hips and where to put my feet and trying to look where I was going whilst keeping my balance, things that your brain normally does without you thinking. Have you ever pulled away from a junction in the wrong gear, or had a dream where you try to run or move and can't? Now apply that to everything and this was now my real world. It's one thing lying on a bed with your brain telling you it will be no problem, but actually trying to do it with your body saying 'no way' is completely different. I was having to think about every little movement, things we all take for granted and thousands of signals out of the millions were getting lost between my brain and my everywhere else. Always listen to your body, don't let your brain trick you with visions of the past. I would definitely need more practice at this, it was hard work to get to the door and I was knackered but I hadn't finished the purpose of my journey yet. I was offered help in the toilet but this was something I had to do myself, surely I could manage this and have the dignity of privacy and I declined the help. I was told there was a big red cord by the toilet, just pull it if there's any problem. I went in, sat down and kept staring confidently with one eye at the big red cord. Right, surely I knew what to do next? I passed what felt like a twenty foot rope with enough girth on it to moor the Titanic. This felt like bliss because I knew it was another system that was working, but then came the confusing bit. I couldn't work out how to wipe my arse. For fuck's sake what's wrong with me? I knew I had to do it but I couldn't work out how to, that's when I knew I was really ill, I couldn't work out how to wipe my arse. My co-ordination and muscle movement between my brain and my hands had completely gone for the moment and I just couldn't think straight. I looked at the big, red cord and thought about it but no, this was something I was going to have to figure out for myself. I managed to do it in the end, it was as if a light had been switched on, power somehow had been rerouted in my head and I managed to wipe my arse, wash my hands and made my way out and back to my bed with the help of the physio, which again was a very slow process and took ages. The doctor was right, it was way too soon.

For me, recovering from my stroke was similar to the way you reboot your computer. You have loads of systems that are coming back online after someone has pulled the plug out. The difference is your brain is so complex, it isn't just a case of pulling the plug out or flicking the on/ off button and ten minutes later, hey presto. No the human brain is far more complex and adaptable than any machine with cogs and flashing lights. Some systems take days, weeks, months maybe years, maybe never to reboot. Sometimes it just felt like my battery was loose. Something wouldn't work but then I'd get a strange sensation and something would ignite, a connection or something, and I'd be able to do it. Your patience and resolve will be tested to the limit but it's your best qualities that get you through and you have to keep thinking of how it will be further down the long winding lane. Your brain is an amazing piece of kit. It soaks up millions of pieces of information at once and adapts to what we think is normal. It's how we grow, learn and develop as babies, to children, to adults. It's just some of us have to do it more than once in our lives. There will be loads you can do from muscle memory but even more that you can't, yet.

The next day, after a brief discussion with the doctors, I was asked if I wanted to have a short walk out of the ward to the end of the corridor and back. Damn right I did. I think the doctors wanted to build on this incredible start and I was eager to try and get up and about and I wanted a change of scenery. I wasn't going to improve lying on my back and after yesterday's trip to the toilet I felt strong enough and ready, but I was also apprehensive and ready to listen to my body and not be tricked by my brain. No I definitely felt strong enough for a short walk with the physio. Out came my drips, off came my leg pads and

I swung my legs off the bed in search of my new slippers. This time I knew what to expect, just shut one eye, take it easy and listen. It was only about twenty yards to a big set of double doors at the end of the ward but to me it could have been twenty miles. I slowly shuffled up to the end of the ward with the physio on my arm, this was ridiculously early in my recovery but all concerned, including me, felt confident I could do it. It took a good twenty minutes to get to the doors. My balance was seriously poor, it was like I was on a boat. I kept veering to the left, the same as if I was pushing one of those bastard shopping trollies with a stiff wheel. I was asked frequently if I needed a rest but each time I said no and clumped one heavy foot in front of the other. I had one eye shut the whole time and with no depth perception I had no real idea how far away the doors were. The best option was to look at the floor, it's easier to see roughly how many square tiles are in front of you than try to work out distances in mid air. The physio was as pleased as I was when we got to the doors. She pushed them open and we walked outside into another corridor. To me it felt like the outside world and I felt an amazing rush of euphoria, until I turned around.

We had to head back to the safety of my bed, this was enough for one day so we both turned around to make the journey back. My eye automatically saw the sign above the door. It had a name or something followed by 'Acute Stroke Ward'. At that point I felt the colour drain out of my face, my legs felt weak and I could feel the questions building up, how bad? How long? However, keep focused, I was still twenty odd yards from safety, let's get back first. Everything had again just become a little more serious.

I got back to my bed and felt absolutely knackered, completely exhausted and an overwhelming feeling of this is not your normal hospital visit. So far I had been trying to convince everyone I was better than I actually was, the medical team, my family, the kids, visitors, even myself. Seeing that sign above the door had removed all doubt for me, I am ill. I also had a bastard of a headache. My eyes were so achy, using them alternatively and having to scowl and concentrate for the longest stint yet. I can only liken it to a hangover, I've had enough of them in my life to know what I'm talking about. I spoke with one of the ward staff about it who came up with a cracking idea. He took one of those cheap, blue, hospital sleeping masks and cut one of the eyes off. I put it on and felt a massive burst of relief. It meant I could see through one eye and see one image but keep both eyes open and my face could relax behind the mask. Ingenious.

The next few days were spent asking myself loads of questions. How long am I going to be in here? Is this permanent? How long is this going to last? Will I still be able to support my family? My confidence was shot on so many levels, I'd go to move and couldn't, I'd tried to talk and couldn't, I'd try to see and couldn't. Every morning I would wake up and look across the room to see if by some miracle my sight had returned, every morning started with a piece of disappointment. I was sleeping loads for long periods at strange times. Your brain works on so many things at once that it will shut down as much of you as possible in order to repair. Even while you sleep it is still running your breathing, your heart and your digestive system. The less it has to do the more it can concentrate on repair so it puts you to sleep. To repair it needs nutrients. I was craving food, clock watching for meal times but this wasn't satisfying my growing appetite. I started asking the porters if there were any spare meals left at dinner. After a while they started bringing me extra dinners and evening meals without asking, which I had to keep quiet from the nurses but we all got a major bollocking when matron found out as I was supposed to be watching my salt and sugar intake. Instead of looking at the 'how to' manual, I was listening to my body.

I was now allowed to get up and go the toilet and shower room by myself. Those pads on my legs had been removed and I had been for a couple of walks with the physio, including one outside. This was a little walk around a small uneven paved area, different to the smooth, level hospital corridors to see how I handled unfamiliar surroundings. This also included a trip up and down a flight of stairs which again took me a lot of getting used to, using different muscle groups, completely different to walking on a flat surface. This was helping me to be more mobile but there was one burning question I had to know.

It was after a few days, I needed to know the answer to the biggest question I have ever asked myself, am I still a man? My missus came to visit early in the morning and I asked if she would come into the shower room with me. We stripped off, we had a shower together and then I answered my question. I claim to be the only person in the world to have full sex, as a patient, in the toilets of the acute stroke ward in St George's. Classy. This is not some sort of brag or trophy and I'm not going into details, but I needed to know if I was still going to be the man that could satisfy my woman. I was and afterwards I gave her a hug and it was the most loving, electric hug we have ever shared with each other. While we're on the subject, I just want to put it on record officially that I never had a problem in that area, happily that part of me was never affected.

Knowing this I now wanted to go home. I felt half ready, even though physically I probably wasn't, but I wouldn't be on my own at home and I had age on my side. I asked to go as soon as I could, the doctors were happy with the amazing progress I had made in such a short space of time, but was it safe for me to go home? It was a Sunday morning and I was given a small task to complete which would determine if they would even think about letting me go home. I wasn't going to fail. I had to go down a flight a stairs to a small canteen and make myself a cup of tea and some toast. That was it, sounds so easy but for me this was massive. I put on my eye patch, got suitably dressed and tried to remember everything I felt from my previous little walks. It was so hard, I was concentrating so hard with one eye it hurt but I passed so now they could think about letting me out. This was a huge gamble for all including me, this was less than a week since my life had nearly ended, but thankfully I was given the green light to leave. I got ready as quick as my slowness would let me and I thanked as many of the fantastic staff as I could. I'm sure most of them weren't born on planet Earth. To have so much care, friendship, a will to help, humility, support, patience and professionalism, surely they must be from another planet?? I despise those that knock the NHS. I was ready for the start of the rest of my life. I put on my clothes and grabbed my big bag of assorted medication. As I walked out, I looked around at the others still in bed and for the first time in my life I felt age was on my side. I wished my ward mates all the very best and hoped sincerely that soon they would be able to walk out the same way I was about to.

CHAPTER FOUR

Back Home

I got out of the cab with the missus and looked at the front door with one eye. I was so relieved to be home but I knew I had been extremely lucky and this was going to be the start of a long, difficult journey. I had been signed off work for the forseeable future so what was my role at home now? Had I come out of hospital too soon? I certainly didn't think so and the doctors were happy to let me go, always trust the experts but there was still that bit of denial in me that thought I was going to be back at work in a couple of months or so. The truth is I had no idea what was in store or how long it would be before I could return to work and my life of routine. There was a lot of anxiety at first when I walked in and stood in front of the kids, I was home, I was ill but I didn't want them knowing how ill I really was. I was still me, this pillar that was always there for them but kids know instinctively when something is wrong and my right eye was starting to point up in the air which was a big giveaway. I went straight in and after some big, loving hugs I went up to bed, steadily and purposely up the stairs one at a time, putting on a stage show of strength and resilience for the small pairs of eyes that were watching me. I lay down on our bed and then the most beautiful thing happened.

The youngest came in and stuck two pictures up on the wall above the bed where I was laying up to my left. One was a lovely butterfly and the other was a mad dinosaur both drawn when she was three years old at playschool. She had been told my eyes were not working properly so looking at these lovely innocent pictures with their bright colours would help me get better and she gave me a massive hug. I tried to move my eyes around to them, I couldn't see them but they looked so beautiful. I lay down on the bed and had a look round and everything that was so familiar suddenly looked so different. I knew this room so well but because I had no depth perception or peripheral vision, everything looked as if it had been moved around and squashed together. Hospital was different, I didn't know it any better but I knew home, I just couldn't recognize it. Things that I knew were close suddenly appeared far away and vice versa and I knew that from now on I couldn't rely on trusting my eyes. This bed and this bedroom was going to be my safe area from now on.

I looked past my feet towards the door to our bathroom, which was now two doors and I tried desperately to get the two images to merge. I couldn't so I tried something smaller, the light fitting dead ahead at the end of the room. It felt like my eyes were going to burst but no joy with that either. Surely this would get better quickly now I was at home. I tried then to move my eyes top left to see the butterfly and the dinosaur but had to cheat by turning my head. My eyes were just not playing ball and this was to become my routine hour upon hour upon hour for months to come, door frame, light fitting, butterfly, dinosaur, repeat.

Maybe it would be better tomorrow, or later today perhaps. This daily exercise routine contributed to my constant headache but I wanted to see properly. My missus was thinking a lot more realistically and she got a second job in case I could never go back to work. She seemed to be working around the clock and I warned her that if she didn't take her foot off the pedal then she would end up in the same condition as me. I understood though it wasn't just work for her, it was both support for our family and probably a bit of escape for her, away from the demands of the kids and myself. I did feel lonely though. I wanted to talk about what had happened, I wanted reassurance everything was going to be as normal, answers that I did not and could not impose on the kids. I needed someone to bounce off as it is a very lonely place in your own head. Never be too proud or embarrassed to ask for help or to talk it out. Help is all around you, even from the most unlikely sources, even if the answer isn't.

I wanted my routines at home to be as similar as I could get them to my time in hospital. I ate at exactly the same time as I did in hospital, took my medication the same time, even trying to go to the toilet at roughly the same time. I dare not miss a tablet time or worse still, run out of them. My confidence was so low on so many levels I was petrified that if I strayed from this routine then my body would shut down again. I was told to reduce my sugar and salt intake whilst I was in hospital. It didn't bother me at the time because I had never really been a big fan of either. I'd never taken sugar in my tea of coffee and I'd never put extra salt on my dinner, except perhaps on the odd portion of chips from the chippy. I had never worried about my intake of either but the moment I got home and tried to watch it, my taste buds got paranoid and I could taste salt and sugar in everything. If no one had mentioned it then I would never had tasted it but now it tasted as if everything I ate had massive doses of both in it. So I started eating only low salt and low sugar food options. I was bought some low salt peanut butter to have on some toast as a treat and I even once tried some of that vegetarian meat in a Bolognese, once. I'm sorry, that's not for me. I'm sure it's very good for you and some will swear by it but I just swore at it. For me there's nothing like biting into a medium cooked meat like a thick steak or juicy pork chop, this was like eating plastic, no more ever again and that was to be the end of my diet change. Nothing I ate had determined my stroke and I've always been a believer that if you're hungry then your body is telling you to have something so eat. Some people in the world don't have that luxury.

I was starting to feel hungry at different times, I figured it was my body telling me it needed nutrients to help repair. The same applies with sleeping although one thing I did change was the way round I slept in bed. Me and the missus had our bedroom at the top of the stairs and the kids had to walk past there to get to their rooms or downstairs. We slept with our heads visible from the doorway so the kids had some reassurance for whatever reason and we could see out and knew if they were up but in the first few weeks I was worried that if I had another stroke and died, then the first thing they would see would be my face, dead in bed. That would haunt them for the rest of their lives so I turned round so all you could see from the doorway was my feet. Yes, my missus did turn round too. I returned to my normal position for door frame, light fitting, butterfly, dinosaur. I would get really tired really quickly in the early weeks of recovery and sleep almost instantly for hours at different times. As I've mentioned before, your brain is already trying to deal with loads of information such as your blood pressure, digestion and breathing so why does it have to worry about talking, looking, thinking, listening, scratching your arse, etc? It will shut down as much as possible to give it a chance to heal itself. Just let it.

I remembered I had a ticket for Arsenal v Manchester City in the Community Shield at Wembley in a few days time. I'd seen them loads of times at the old Wembley but this was going to be first time seeing them at the new Wembley. I resigned myself to the fact there was no way I was going to be able to make it so sadly but with good intention I gave my ticket away to someone who I knew would enjoy it and looked forward to watching it through one eye that weekend on the telly. As you can imagine, I hadn't been able to or felt like watching the telly. Up until now I had been content to plug my headphones into my laptop, shut my eyes and listen to music. I've always had a wide range of music tastes and was currently in my retro stage. There's nothing like a good tune to stir the emotions, bring back a memory of good times and help you try and forget a raging headache or the facts of current reality. The problem was trying to move my eyes around the keyboard, I knew where the letters were roughly but my eyes and fingers couldn't get there so typing was slow and really ached, even with one eye. Anyway I was going to try a bit of telly. I came downstairs just before kick off to watch the big screen in the front room for the first time, settled down leaning slightly to my left, shut my right eye and searched through the channels to find the match. That's harder than you think if your eyes don't move because the channel pages on satellite scroll down very discreetly like a curtain rolling down and your eyes follow it without you thinking. My eyes were on fire and my brain was scrambled before a ball had been kicked, even with me changing left eye to right eye and back again, but I found the correct channel and settled down to watch the game. It was no good, the screen was far too quick for either of my eyes to keep up with, I just couldn't follow the ball. The camera was moving too fast for my stiff eyes to keep up with so had to settle for shutting my eyes and listening to the commentary but this is limited with nothing to see. Where's the damn ball? Who's attacking? Who's on the ball now? I gave up and went back upstairs to safety. I decided I was going to listen to it on the radio, the same way I used to listen to mid week matches when I was a kid. When I was young I had an AM radio which was shaped like an old black 1970's formula one racing car with all the old, gold retro JPS cigarette livery on it. I used to listen to mid week matches on it, hiding it under my bed sheets when I was supposed to be asleep for school in the morning, trying to stay desperately quiet especially if it was an Arsenal game and they scored. I plugged my headphones clumsily into my laptop and tuned in to the match. What a difference, suddenly I was at the game. The big difference between radio and tv commentary is that radio is more intricate due to there being no visuals to fall back on. Now I knew where the ball was, the action was described in more detail and I could get more into the game, hats off to all radio sports commentators who get a bit more respect from me from now on. I recall at the start of that season that Tottenham had a really good start and at one point early on they were top of the table. I remember seeing a screenshot of the Premier League table with Tottenham on top and I thought 'Oh no, my eyes must be properly fucked!'

The other thing I couldn't do properly was read, this was a real weird one and I learnt that reading is not just recognizing words. When you learn to read as a child, part of the learning is that your right eye automatically knows where the end of the line is and your left eye is ready to drop down to the next line. I had lost this simple function so I kept reading the same line over and over and over again. I just thought it was because of my stiff eyes and it drove me insane, the very definition of frustrating, especially when I kept reading the name of the horse over and over and was unable to drop down to read the name of the trainer and the jockey. Even though I could read, I had to learn to read again.

I only came out of my safe area a few times in the first few weeks, mainly either to use the bathroom or the kitchen with the regular trip back with my Dad to the hospital. I lay there in bed for hours doing my exercise routine, door frame, light fitting, butterfly, dinosaur, trying desperately to get my eyes to move more easy and hopefully get rid of this head fuck double vision which would in turn rid me of this bastard headache. I also had to go back to hospital regularly both to neurology and the eye department for my checkups. It was during one of my early checkups in neurology that I hit possibly the biggest milestone, a real 'switch on' moment. I was in a room, sat at a table with a doctor watching, with a load of building blocks on them. I had to put the blocks one on top of the other with my left hand to build a tower, the same way you see a toddler do when at play. I failed miserably, I had poor co-ordination so my left hand was all over the place and my lack of depth perception meant I had no idea where the stack was that I was looking at. I was dropping blocks on the floor, on the table, knocking blocks over, it was ridiculous and I felt so embarrassed and stupid. Frustrated and humiliated I swept the blocks off the table with my arm and shouted 'Fucking hell, this is crazy, I can't do this!' The doctor put his hand on my shoulder and with a quiet, calming voice he said 'You can't do this, yet'. This three letter word, yet, was the biggest word I had ever heard. I used to think it was 'if', if only I'd done my lottery numbers, if only I'd done it this way, if only we'd scored that last minute penalty. It was now 'yet'. Everything I couldn't do I just couldn't do, yet. You can apply this to so many things in your life, just tell yourself you haven't done it, yet. Accepting this huge word was so important in my recovery to come and a word I want to pass on to anyone who finds themselves in a similar situation to me.

The next big milestone happened after around five weeks. I woke up and everything seemed so much bigger and brighter. It took me a couple of moments to realise that my peripheral vision had come back on my right side as if by magic. My world had now got an extra thirty percent bigger. Everything was now in widescreen and this was the point that I knew my body was fighting it and this gave me such a lift. It was September and it was the first point at which I knew I was making a real go at getting better and more importantly I still had it in me. Up to this point it had felt very much like let's go with the flow and see what happens but this was incredible. I still had nothing on my left, yet. That would take another two weeks to return to have full widescreen and I still had this crazy double vision but this was such a massive change for me and I couldn't wait to tell my family.

Every so often, a visit to the hospital was followed by a visit to work to hand in an updated sicknote. It would always involve a lift as walking any distances was way too soon and I actually looked forward to this, to have a chance of seeing other people I knew and a chance to be in familiar surroundings that I knew really well. It was also my way of saying 'I'm still about, I'm still fighting this and improving and I'll be back soon hopefully'. Perhaps it was also my way of trying to convince myself that I would be back soon, to expel any sub conscious doubt that I had buried in my head. My Dad would give me a lift in and would help me into the building and then I would take over. I knew the layout, I knew the floor was level so this compensated for my lack of depth perception. I'd put on my glasses or just shut one eye and make my way upstairs to hand in my paperwork. I thought I was doing ok but I remember struggling downstairs once, along one of the corridors and walking out into one of the back areas. I saw two familiar faces stood still looking at me and with one eye shut I said hello. I could tell by the looks on their faces and their hesitation in their reply that I was not the person they knew before, yet. One visit was over Halloween so I picked up some pumpkins with the two youngest which I thought I could help them carve out. These were huge and I needed their help even to pick them up, I thought at one point a tomato would be more my level. It was around this time that I made a tongue in cheek declaration on social media that after consulting with my agent and the medical team it was with great sadness and reluctance that I was retiring from international football with immediate effect. A couple of England players had declared this recently after being dropped. Amazing how they think in their world. They call it their decision to retire, I call it someone else's decision to drop or sack them.

It's true what they say about how other things or parts of your body start to compensate for other areas that are either damaged or missing. My eyesight was poor and out of real time but my hearing became super sharp. I don't know if that was because I was so reliant on it now or if it was my brain turning up the levels to compensate for my eyes. I could actually hear a pin drop and my head was alert and would turn and be drawn to face different sounds. I reckon if you called me a bastard from any corner of London then I would have heard you and I started to become a lot more reliant on my ears than my eyes. A whole new world is out there if you can hear it, things that normally your brain filters out in the day to day hustle bustle. Your eyes try to be extremely dominant but there's loads you can't see. Try it sometime, just stop everything and listen.

I was always taught as a kid that if you're going to do something then do it properly first time. Think it through beforehand so you don't make any stupid mistakes. This had been instilled in me since as long as I can remember. In some respects it felt like I was a young child again trying to learn things but with an adult memory telling me I already knew how to do it. What I was learning is that sometimes good enough is good enough. Perhaps I was never going to recover back to how I was before the stroke so try not to sacrifice the moment. Of course you should look forward, or backward for that matter, but don't stare. I felt like I was getting a bit stronger and with my hearing on full power and my peripheral vision back on my left side, I felt confident enough to try and introduce myself back somewhere in the big outside.

CHAPTER FIVE

Back Into The Wild Of Reality

Weeks on end confined to the same room for large chunks of your time was starting to take it's toll on me and I needed some fresh scenery. I've never been one for sitting around and I needed to see what else I was capable of. I'd tried to have a few sessions at home on my electric guitar but it was no good. I'd started having lessons about two years ago, ironic that I wanted to try and learn something new to stop my brain turning to jelly in my old age, then I go and have a stroke. I could play a few riffs and a few tunes that I used to practice but my hand co-ordination and my muscle memory in my fingers had gone. I just couldn't seem to play anything that I used to know so well, yet. I couldn't even look at the strings properly, there seemed to be loads of them and they moved all over the place. No, I wanted to get out and about, to show that I wasn't washed up and finished. I had my determination and pride but I was still finding out what I couldn't do but only when I went to do it. That is so frustrating. Things you know and can remember you've done without thinking for decades have now confusingly become impossible because your body doesn't seem to listen. There were systems that were still rebooting still after all this time but now I knew my brain and body were trying and needed a bit of help. My peripheral vision was back on both sides and although my vision was a jumbled mess, my balance was poor and my co-ordination was shit, my hearing was 20/20 and I finally felt confident to have a little walk outside to feel like I was somewhere familiar but different. This was going to be my first trip anywhere beyond the front door on my own since my stroke, but I've never been worried about being any-where on my own. I've visited loads of towns home and abroad, usually football related, usually my own so a short walk round the block should be no problem, surely? The difference was back then I knew I could look after myself, this was now a different ball game.

I had been given two pairs of glasses by the hospital, one with a frosted lense which shut down one eye, and one pair with a prism lense on one side, to try and level out my vision by deflecting one image in a different direction. I opted for the prism lense pair for this milestone as I thought this would make me look more normal to others. Vanity was still getting in the way of practicality. This lense would work to a point but my eyes would move and the images would change position so I would revert to the more trusted 'camera one, camera two' method. I made my way outside to the kerb outside our house, best guess. It was easier for me to judge distances by looking at the ground, I could roughly work out the amount of paving stones between me and the next obstacle but like a fool, to look normal, I was walking and trying to act at the same pace as before my stroke. It didn't take long to be reminded that my brain and reflexes were not as quick and could not keep up. I got to the kerb and felt it with my foot. Even though I could see it I wasn't sure where it was and I didn't want this journey to end after just ten paces. Now our road isn't busy at this time, sure it can be a little rat run during rush hour but this was a quiet mid morning so there wasn't a lot of traffic. Right here goes, crossing the road by myself. Normally there would be someone on my arm leading me but now I was on my own and there was a whole load of old routines I would have to re learn. I looked right and the road was clear but as soon as I looked left I couldn't remember what right looked like. I had looked right but my brain had not registered any of the information my eyes had given it. I had turned my head as usual to look the other way but it had been too quick for my ever changing limits. There's a massive difference between looking and seeing and again I had stumbled across something I couldn't do at the moment of truth. I had to keep looking right, stop, say to myself what I could see, remember it and then do the same for left. This took a while and then the traffic played its joker. A car went past, I heard it, I knew it had passed but I saw it moments later, this threw me completely. My eyes and hearing were still badly out of sync and I remembered not to trust my eyes anymore, just listen. It's true in so many ways that there's none so blind as those that don't listen. I was sure the road was clear and I couldn't hear any cars so I aimed for the other side of the road. One of our neighbours had an electric car that had nearly scooped me up before I was ill. I just hoped there were none of those electric cars about. You can't hear them and you're not used to them being about, they certainly weren't mentioned in the old green cross code. They are really hard to pick up normally when crossing the road and now I was trying to listen out for these silent assasins. How are the elderly or the short sighted going to cross the road in the future? I hadn't even thought about the other silent danger, push bikes. What a pain in the arse most of those were in my recovery. Every cyclist it seems to me wants to be treated the same as everyone else on the road, except of course when it comes to things like traffic lights, T-junctions, crossroads, slow moving traffic, road tax, insurance etc. You wouldn't run full speed up a cycle lane in slow moving traffic then dodge in and out so why do cyclists think it's ok to ride their bike like that at full speed? Twice I've nearly been hit by a cyclist, twice by an idiot trying to beat the slow moving traffic and coming out of nowhere flat out. I remember the old advert 'Think once, think twice, think bike'. If it was up to me, I would make all cyclists take driving lessons, not the test, just lessons so they can read the bloody road and be aware of other road users. Think car, lorry, pedestrian.

Anyway, I had got to the other side of the road and the safety of the pavement, this would be a quick walk round the block as I could now feel the confidence slowly draining out from the bottom of my feet but it was something I had to complete. I was veering heavily to the left, the world was trying to jump up from my right and knock me over and I had to keep adjusting myself and I stopped thinking about looking normal to everyone else. Was this my balance which I knew was poor, or did I genuinely have weakness on my left side? I reckoned I would have been brilliant as a racehorse in the Derby at Epsom. I would hug that sharp left hand bend all the way around Tattenham Corner and romp it up the straight lengths clear. I would be useless at right handed tracks such as Goodwood and Ascot, a real coupon buster as the reigning Derby winner would veer left and end up in one of the car parks. I battled on, short step by short step, concentrating on every little thing I did and trying to take in what was going on around me. You just do not realise how much your brain deals with until part of it's taken away. I made it all the way round the block and back up the main road, probably no more than two hundred yards but it felt like an expedition. It wasn't just the physical exertion, but also the mental awareness, having to concentrate on every little movement and be aware of what and who was around you. I got home back behind the front door and quite literally fell into the chair. I was exhausted, I had nothing left and I fell asleep almost immediately where I sat for a good couple of hours. It was just what I needed and I needed to do more of it, especially in the rain. It was so much easier in the rain because I could hear the traffic move in the wet conditions so much clearer and easier, even the electric cars and the dreaded bikes, plus there were less people about, less moving obstacles to avoid on the pavements. I couldn't wait for it to rain, luckily we get loads of it over here in Autumn and I started to feel more and more confident on my little walks. I tried to make them a bit longer each time without being stupid to try and build up my strength mentally and physically. If was going to be back at work at Christmas I had an awful lot to do. My brain and body needed practice doing the simple, if I couldn't do the simple then how was I going to achieve the more difficult. It was during one of my walks in the rain that the unthinkable happened, something I was just not prepared for. I was in a good rhythm about two hundred yards from the front door when the sun came out. It was like a nuclear bomb had exploded overhead and it changed my view from my eyes completely. My vision at this point was a mixture of blurry and double but the sun had thrown a new element into the mix for me to deal with. The bright sunshine was reflecting off the wet surfaces at all angles and I had to stop. My vision had suddenly turned into this funky, psychedelic kaleidoscope vision. Everything it seemed now had multiple images, the sort of thing I could imagine a spider seeing and I just couldn't process this information. It was very trippy so I covered one eye and drudged back to the safety behind the front door for more door frame, light fitting, butterfly, dinosaur. This new twist threw a spanner in the works, perhaps I wasn't ready for the big outside, yet? I would have to take note of the weather forecast more carefully from on.

This didn't deter me for long though and I started getting braver again. I was desparate to get out as much as possible. If I was going to return to work soon then I needed to practice a wider variety of things such as getting on and off the tube, interacting with other people and using a ticket barrier so one morning I decided I was going to take a trip, just one stop, on the tube. I was going to try the normal journey I used to make to work just to see if I could do it as I was so much better at thinking and moving in familiar surroundings. This was definitely going to require the frosted lense pair of glasses, I'd practically given up on the prism lense anyway because if felt like my eyes had moved past the point that the prism was correcting so let's see if I could try and act at normal speed and blend in with the rest of society. With a mixture of enthusiasm and apprehension, I headed down to the tube station. This would involve a distance similar to my walk around the block, then crossing the busy main high street. This time I was taking no chances crossing the main road by guesswork and I waited for the beep, beep, beep at the pedestrian crossing. I approached the tube station and had to stop. A tube must have just pulled in and a crowd of people swarmed out of the station onto the high street and into my flight path, all going about their daily business. I could see all these people but I had no idea where they were or how far away they were it was just too much information to process at once so I backed up out the way against one of the shop windows. They were all going in different directions at different speeds and I felt like the Millenium Falcon in The Empire Strikes Back when it's travelling through the asteroid field. If I carried on then I would bump into numerous people,

I found out very quickly that I couldn't handle crowds, yet. It felt like there were bodies coming at me from all angles, yet I seemed to be the only one who was looking where they were going. Everyone else had their eyes firmly planted on their mobile phones, walking around as if on autopilot, taking where they're supposed to be going for granted and none of them had a clue what was going on around them in the world. It seems to me that most people's mobile phone is nothing more than electronic heroin. There's a huge difference between looking where you're going and being aware what's going on around you and this lot seemed to be doing neither and it is becoming so increasingly common. I remember shouting at the telly during the run up to the last general election when that mathmetician tried to convince everybody that we needed another ten thousand police officers that could go out and talk to people. Really?? Why not just tell eight and a half million Londoners to put their phones down, take their earphones out and have a look at what's going on around them. Then you can save the extra money or spend it on the NHS. If you want the definition of an easy target then just look at your average person in rush hour on their phones, it's frightening. The stupid of the future.

So as you can tell I already had the hump but onward ho and the best was yet to come. I was starting to have second thoughts, the world was moving too quick for me but no, I was going to carry on. What's the worst that can happen with all these people about? I waited for the crowd to subside, got my Oyster card ready and went to negotiate the ticket barrier. I wanted to look as normal as possible so I walked towards it at what I thought was a normal speed. It did seem to come at me really quickly so I slowed a bit and I could sense someone really close behind me. The fare dodger, a familiar thing on the underground, had singled me out to pay for his journey. He must have seen that maybe I was struggling and as I slowed to go through the barrier, he shuffled in behind, went through with me nearly in my pocket and kicked me straight on the back of the Achilles for good measure, the one I had snapped years earlier. The pain rocketed up my leg and the guy just went straight past me in silence towards the top of the escalator. I was fucking livid, perhaps it was weeks of pent up frustration spilling out at once but the idiot in me came racing to the surface. I went after him, go now, think later and even with my double vision I was locked on. His ignorance suggested to me that he wasn't expecting a response, oh really? 'Oi you ignorant wanker!' I shouted and squared up to him with my frosted glasses on at the top of the moving escalator. My next fear in this journey was to have been getting on the moving downward escalator but my anger had just overridden it and I was on it without thinking. He turned to me and said so casually 'Did you just call me a wanker?' I could feel my blood boiling and all my old emotions came roaring out. 'No I called you an ignorant wanker! Have you got no fucking manners? Can't you even say sorry?' I shouted. At this point I became aware of two things. Firstly I could feel everyone on both the up and down escalators looking at me hoping for a bit of morning tube rage action. I was local so there must have been people there that recognized me. Secondly and perhaps more importantly, I was at the top of a steep moving escalator, with double vision, no balance or co-ordination, fronting up quite a big fella. I thought briefly if he goes for it I've got no chance. If I even take a swing and miss with my bad eyesight then I'm going down this escalator headfirst, but I'm not losing face here. Quietly and with some sincerity, he just looked at me pathetically and said 'Sorry mate, I need to get somewhere and I'm potless' and my anger dropped a load of notches very quickly and for a split second I nearly offered him a couple of quid. Another example of thinking I could do something that I couldn't follow through. My sensible side had returned quicker than normal and probably saved me from a fall down the escalator, a smack in the mouth and a probable broken neck. Idiot, I thought. I need to think a lot clearer and remember my limits. I got down to the platform no problem and onto the first carriage of the tube. I was in no condition to try and negotiate the ignorant pairs of legs that never move for you, spread across the carriage so I just stood at the end and held on for the short journey. You might have already guessed that I hate travelling on the tube.

This wasn't the end of my journey though. My confidence was at a new high so where else could I go? Instead of turning round and going back home, I came out of the tube station and headed to the small shopping centre for a quick look around. Still with one eye shut, I made my way up the short walk and into one of the large stores, the blue one that sounds like footwear. I wanted to buy something for the missus, not sure what, perhaps a bottle of perfume or some beauty products, just something that would help take her away from reality for a while. I walked in and I could see an end of products that looked as if they might be on special offer. As I walked towards it, there was an almighty crash and products were rolling across the sales floor. I couldn't judge the distance of any of the shelving and I had walked straight into one of their promotional ends that my eyes had tricked me into thinking they were further away. I was so embarrassed, I bet everyone thought I was probably drunk, so I started to try and grab the various items that were rolling around the floor. This probably made it look worse as moving items were even harder to place so there was a lot of grabbing thin air. One of the staff came up to me and my face must have been the colour of a beetroot. I explained to the very kind and sympathetic lady that I wasn't drunk or under the influence of anything but was recovering from a stroke and my vision was extremely poor. Instead of just agreeing with me she told me her father had suffered a stroke and was having to deal with a similar thing so she understood exactly what I was going through. I didn't want her to understand, to understand meant she would have had to go through what I went through. You would then understand how I was feeling and what I was looking at. I mean this honestly and sincerely, I wouldn't wish this on my worst enemy. This means, for all the right reasons, I don't want anyone to understand how I feel! I wasn't too proud to accept the help offered though. My embarrassment quickly turned to a sense of relief, I had someone on my side against the multiple pairs of watching eyes, the eyes that do just that instead of helping, someone who could explain to others what was happening. Despite my high confidence earlier in the day, it had taken an abrupt battering and I realized I wasn't ready for shopping, yet.

I wanted to do something for my Dad. He had been checking up on me every day since my stroke, making sure I was alright in myself, making sure I wasn't short of money being off work, giving me lifts to all my hospital appointments and just being there, the same as he always had been all my life. I wanted to do something different and I came up with probably the worst idea possible. I had already determined that I could not handle crowds but still I got a pair of tickets for Arsenal's next Champion's League game which I knew my Dad would appreciate. It had been years since we had gone to football together, probably not since we sat together in the North Bank at Highbury and as much as it was a gift for my Dad, it was also another big test and hurdle for me. Anyone with any sense would have told you this is madness, going to mix with a sixty thousand plus crowd just over three months since my lights nearly permanently went out. Football though is in my blood, I'd been going for the best part of forty years and I knew the journey and territory well. Complete madness!

My Dad came to meet me, I put on my glasses and my 1979 cup final replica shirt. It is the yellow one and I've got a blue number seven on it after my first hero as a kid. Connoisseurs will have already recognized it on the front cover of this book I hope. I always wear that shirt because I identify more with the old days at Highbury on the North Bank rather than this new corporate era at the Emirates. We got on the busy rush hour tube and my Dad kept grabbing my arm and leading me in the right direction as the amount of people about had confused me and was just too much for me to take in. I was wandering all over the place, I was going every direction but straight. I could tell my Dad thought this was a bad idea and he asked me if we should give it a miss, it was on the telly anyway if we wanted to watch it. No, we were going on, I wasn't going to back out now plus tickets up there as you know aren't cheap. We got to Finsbury Park station, awash with red and white moving objects that I tried to avoid and we walked across the station front to cross the road. I went to cross the road and my Dad just grabbed a handful of the back of my coat and dragged me back out of the way of the oncoming traffic. The loud horn and two big, bright headlights on full beam on this quick moving lump of metal were urgently reminding me that I did not have priority to cross at the moment. I'm sure the sign was green, perhaps it had changed to red and it hadn't registered, perhaps I was looking at the wrong sign? Where is the sign? Why is this so hard? Everything was suddenly so different and not so familiar, the traffic, the movement, the lights and the world started it's timely spin from the right. My Dad helped me across the road with the crowd by taking my arm and leading me like an elderly man, down the short walk towards the Emirates, stopping briefly for the compulsory burger from the usual first van on the left. My Dad was looking at me again with that look I could read, are you sure you want to go through with this? I was sure he wanted us to turn back for my own safety, he knew more than anybody that this was a bad idea but I think he could see how much this achievement would mean to me and that's the only reason he let us both carry on. A short walk later and we arrived at the stadium, I was starting to get used to the amount of people around and made our way over the railway and in. This was the bit I had forgotten about. I always go top tier, you get a much better view in my opinion, but it's a climb up quite a few flights of steps. A walk around the block on the relatively flat surface is one thing but did I have the strength to get up all these steps. There's only one way to find out.

I was absolutely knackered at the top, it took everything out of me and I nearly fell through the big double doors at the top. I was breathing like an asthmatic pit pony but I had done it without stopping so although slower, I must be getting stronger. This definitely warrants a couple of beers before we take our seats I thought to myself so it was my turn to take over and I led my Dad to the bar for some much needed refreshment. We're not there yet though. I saw the big block number in double vision above the entrance we needed but that was about as far as I could manage on my own. Everything again became incredibly fast and confusing. No it wasn't the beer but I had that feeling that you get when the world feels on top of you. Had my brain done too much already? Was my body about to shut down because it had done enough for today? Everything was spinning again and I couldn't read the numbers on either the rows on the floor or the seats to find out where we were sitting and steps to negotiate, as I've explained, are no good with double vision. I had to let my Dad take over again and he led me down the short flight of steps to our seats. He took my hand and led me to my seat the same way he had probably did nearly forty years earlier at Highbury as a wide eyed seven year old. I felt really weird, not embarrassed but more like I was sticking out like a sore thumb. Once in our seats I tried to work out the players that were out for the pre match warm up. Forget that, I could barely see the pitch let alone the players and I couldn't make out anything beyond the half way line. I had to rely on my ears to find out what was happening in the game, trying to listen to the crowd to at least work out the highlights. Like I said, I identify more with the old Highbury crowds than the Emirates and all I'm going to say is that I would have had a better idea what was going on from those good old Highbury crowds on the terraces than with this new 'corporate event' crowd. Arsenal had blown a three goal lead and we left a couple of minutes before the end as the end of match crowd would have been far too much for me to handle, both getting out of the stadium and on the packed station platforms. Apart from the result, the fact I couldn't see sod all or the fact I was nearly run over before the game, I had a great time and felt I had got over an incredible hurdle. It felt like I was retraining my brain and body, getting them used to dealing with what I knew I already had been doing for years, although in hindsight it was way, way too early. I was getting a bit stronger and football has always been in my blood but I was nowhere near ready for a return to the football match experience, yet.

CHAPTER SIX

My Darkest Day

You experience massive highs and lows during your recovery from any serious illness. The lows are born out of frustration and impatience and the extremes can be intense. During one of my check ups at hospital, I had been handed a questionnaire to fill out honestly. It had questions such as 'Do you worry about how others perceive you or look at you?' and 'Have you ever worried about xyz?' etc. I didn't realize it at the time but it was a test to see if I was suffering from depression which is extremely common among stroke sufferers. I just flippantly put two lines through my test and wrote on the back 'I'm only worried that the kids aren't upset' and handed it back in.

The truth is I was suffering with depression but was in so much denial I couldn't admit it. If only I hadn't been so flippant with the questionnaire, if only I wasn't so proud or pig headed. It was only months later when someone explained it to me exactly how depression can feel that I admitted to myself, yes, I did have depression. It creeps up on you gradually in stealth mode and grabs you by the throat without you even knowing. Remember, help is all around you from sometimes the most unlikely sources, friends, family, workmates, professionals, you only have to ask. Help is all around you, even if the answer isn't.

It was one miserable day in November that I reached my lowest point. I was at home in bed, the other half was at work, the kids were at school and I was on my own doing my routine, door frame, light fitting, butterfly, dinosaur which was still failing badly. I still had this bastard headache and double vision which was now entering it's fourth month and I was now past the normal time that I had been told for my body to heal naturally. You see I never took any painkillers, I didn't want them, I thought I could ride this out. Also I didn't want to be in the position of taking two today, two tomorrow, three a day next week, then the next week I'm screaming 'Where's my painkillers?' My headache was like a typical hangover headache and I was now seriously thinking this is as good as it's going to get. I was so, so low and alone. I can't stand it anymore, what if I can never go back to work? I won't be able to look after shit feeling like this, let alone provide for the family. It can be very lonely inside your own head, so with no one but the noise of the rain on the window for company, I made the decision to sort it.

I remember getting showered and dressed really quickly and I double checked my work's pension plan to see if I was still in it in case anything went wrong. Get out the house quick before I change my mind was my mentality, and I walked a very lonely figure, rain soaked but with a sense of relief, all the way down to Wimbledon station which I had worked out would be the easiest and most accessible way to do it. I got to the station and paused for a moment for a quick last look round before going inside. It'll all be over soon.

I went down onto platform eight which I know well even though what I wanted to do would have to take place on empty platform number seven. The plan was to stick my head out slightly in front of the fast train that goes through to Woking through that platform and that would smash my cheekbone which would end my hangover style headache and hopefully end my double vision. It would let the pain out like letting the air out of a balloon. What a fucked up plan, eh? Do not deny or underestimate depression!

I walked right down past the waiting room on platform eight and tried to look normal. I couldn't have stood on platform seven because that is always empty and I would have stuck out like a sore thumb. I kept looking at the floor trying not to catch anybody's eye and waited for the next fast train to come through. Typically there were a lot of people on the station that day or that's what it felt like and I became very paranoid thinking I was being watched on CCTV by the incident watch team. I thought to myself what if one of the station staff comes up to me and asks me what I'm doing? What the hell do I say? I'll come back another day when there isn't such a big audience I tried telling myself. Surely I was allowed a bit of privacy for this and I started to feel the conflict in me. No, it's now or never, my desperation temporarily won. Surely the staff are trained in these situations and I'm going to get rumbled, they know what to look for, so I started to act like I was late, constantly looking at the electronic boards which I couldn't read properly anyway. Then I heard the announcement to stay clear of platform seven as the next train is not stopping. Here we go, let's just get a feel of how this one goes through and judge the distance and speed.

'Fucking Hell' I thought as the train absolutely thundered through. 'That'll take my head off. Mmmm, not a bad idea that. Fuck it, I'm going to end it. I really can't stand this anymore, I'll jump in front of the next train and I'll be free from pain and frustration and my pension will pay out so the missus and kids will be looked after' and I started looking at possible trajectories. I felt beyond low before when my mum died but this was the first time, apart from when I woke up in hospital, that I had seriously contemplated suicide. I reckoned if I jumped upwards, then the speed of the train and the impact would knock me clean out of the station and into the shops opposite and the town would be brought to a standstill. The station was full of people but I'd never felt so alone. It felt like time had stopped and all noise had stopped as a mark of respect. The next train thundered through and I thought right, next one. I'd worked out how to get over the high barrier on the platform and it was a quick couple of steps then a jump in front of the train. I was now ready, this was it. This bastard is going so quick I won't even know it's hit me. I just leant back against the railings and stared at the track.

I think another two trains went past as I just stared at the track in my own little world. I would start moving into position, then stop as if some magical force was holding me back. I did this for a good half hour or so. I must have stood out like a neon light, surely someone must have noticed? I'm not sure what it was, either the sun coming out or the 'on' switch flicking on in my brain but something changed and I thought this is not for me and I actually started thinking rationally. What about the driver of the train, the team of staff that would have to play hunt the thimble for my body parts on the track? What if I do get smashed up and out the station and either smash into the top deck of a bus, or land on a group of schoolkids going to school? It would definitely injure and probably haunt those poor souls who witnessed it forever. What if my head, without the body attached, went flying through the air and knocked out and killed a pensioner with a headbutt? This is not the way I want to be remembered and I knew I didn't have the bottle to go through with it. Not just that, but was I really going to selfishly and disrespectfully stick two fingers up at the people who had got me this far? The medical team in hospital who had worked tirelessly to bring me back out of death's door, my family who had shown so much love, patience and compassion. No I owed it to them to keep fighting. I realized that it wasn't just me involved, it was a massive team effort and now I was more determined than ever. How low must my Dad have felt when my Mum died? But he remained a pillar of strength for us all. Life throws you some weird twists at times but you have to puff your chest out play the hand you've been dealt.

I walked out of the station with a new attitude and made it clear to myself that I was going to get better. Each day I would improve on the day before, however small an improvement. I thought to myself how desperate must somebody be to actually go through with killing themselves. I then thought I bet pension plans don't pay out on suicide so that would have been a balls up and a complete waste of time. The sun came out and with the reflections on the wet surfaces my vision went all kaleidoscope again. I stopped on the pavement out of everybody's way and noticing the detail in my view looked at how beautiful it was. I put my glasses on and walked back home. Thankfully that was the lowest point I felt during my recovery and those times are well behind me.

CHAPTER SEVEN

Back to Work

I came back from one of my check ups in late November feeling gutted. You see I was hoping to be allowed back to work but I had just been signed off again. Once more I was in denial about how ill I still was but I was convinced I was well enough to still play some sort of role. I wanted to go back for two reasons. Firstly I was getting bored at home. I'm damn impatient and I needed something extra, a part to play in something, a chance to prove I was still the same person. Secondly and much, much more importantly, I had reached a point that I never wanted to get to. I was starting to adjust and get used to my condition instead of getting better. On average, most stroke victims do a majority of their recovery in the first three months. After then, recovery becomes a lot slower and I had already passed this fictional dateline. After six months any further recovery is unusual. I needed extra stimulus to help me get better, I didn't want to just get used to it. Looking back I now realize this was way, way too soon to return to work. My brain was once again tricking me into believing I was better than I actually was and I was putting myself under pressure to return to work. I gave my sick note to my boss and embarrassingly I apologized for having more time off. I was worried about possibly losing my job or not ever being able to return in any sort of capacity. I was doubting everything, who would employ someone in their mid forties who clearly had physical problems? His reply was spectacular. 'Listen mate' he said, 'We sell tins of beans, that's what this job basically is. I'd rather have you back 100 per cent when you're ready rather than you rush yourself back and make yourself ill again.' I'll always thank him for that as it felt like a big weight had just been removed from around my neck. My next appointment was made for three weeks time and I was due to have a heart monitor fitted for seven days. I thought to myself this is my chance, if nothing shows up on this then I'm going to make sure I'm well enough to get signed back to work.

I started walking long distances to try and build my strength and stamina up and to try and get my eyesight to adjust to different surroundings. Sounds quite easy but when you have double vision the world can be quite an obstacle course. I stuck to areas I knew well and went out for miles at a time, always making sure I knew where any shops were in case I needed help. If I was to convince the medical experts I could slip back easily into reality then I needed to be as strong as possible. I felt confident on the day I had my heart monitor fitted. It was nothing like I had imagined, just a box stuck to my chest wired to those rubber conductor pads with the metal nipples, stuck on various areas of my chest and back which gave a read out of my blood flow. As I left, the Doctor reminded me not to do anything too energetic or untoward or I would give it an irregular reading. 'Fat chance of that happening' I thought to myself and off I went for the week. I could take it off in the shower so that was easy and the only problem I had with it is that it's a bastard to try and sleep with it on. You feel like a fucking Dalek. Still that's the least of my problems.

A week later and I was back in hospital for my results and hopefully get the nod I was hoping for. I sat there and it just felt so much better. I'm sure the doctors could tell this too. I was told the reading was clear on my heart monitor and I've never felt relief like it. 'Does this mean I can go back to work?' I asked. 'Yes, as long as you start part- time and take it easy' was the reply and both doctors gave me a massive smile, I think it meant a lot to them too. They wrote me out my final sick note which was until 21st January, which was just under six months since I had my stroke. This meant so much to me. I had something to look forward to and it felt like I had turned another massive corner and I got a lift to work to hand my note in to the bosses. I felt such excitement but I knew I was very fortunate to be given this opportunity.

I got to work with a new found spring in my step and went to tell my news to the bosses. They were in one of the offices and they welcomed me in. I was asked what I thought I could do and to be honest I didn't know. You see I was still hesitating badly and struggling with co- ordination so I wouldn't know what I couldn't do until I tried to do it. Sure my brain would tell me I could do it but would my body respond? My confidence was also shot to pieces. 'Confidence of what?' asked one of them. 'Everything, even sneezing!' I said. 'To be honest I don't care what I do. If you want me to stand in the car park and sweep up dogshit then I'll do that, as long as I'm doing something.' I then realized I hadn't sneezed since my stroke, weird. I was offered a few part time light duty roles and I took the first one, a nice four hour shift five days a week. At no time did any of the bosses put any pressure on me, they let me decide and made it so easy for me and I can't thank them enough for that. The only thing I didn't have was a uniform, mine had been cut off the night lightning struck on the stretcher so I had to get a new one from the stores.

The big day arrived, I'd never looked forward to going to work so much. I grabbed my glasses with one lens blanked out and made my way to work. It was a short four hour shift starting at 4pm but I felt like I had a role to play again as a colleague, a partner, a father and as a man. I was finally back in the human race. I got in and made my way up to the staff room. I felt confident as I knew the place, the floors are flat, I know the layout, I know where the doors are, how high the door handles are and rough distances. Despite the fact I still had little balance, little depth perception and double vision I felt comfortable, right up to the bottom of the stairs. Hang on, who the fuck has done this?

The leading edges of each step had been painted bright yellow, probably some sort of health and safety requirement, but with little balance and double vision it made me feel like I was walking through numerous pairs of yellow, aggressive, moving scissors cutting at my legs and the whole place now felt like I was now at sea in bad weather. Now don't get me wrong, I'm all for a bit of health and safety if it stops serious injury or better still, saves lives. The problem is we have gone completely overboard because a large percentage of people have no common sense, especially in my view, the people in charge of health and safety. I don't need a sign on the floor if it's raining telling me to take care as the floor might be wet. I'll work that out well in advance and make the necessary adjustment to my walking speed. If I fall over, it won't be because I haven't read the sign, it'll be because I haven't used common sense or looked where I was going. I wish some people would realize that sometimes it's their fault rather than constantly looking for someone else to blame for their own stupidity. I was recently at the tube station and an announcement went out to please mind your step as due to adverse weather the surfaces may be slippery. It's Autumn, it's England and it's called drizzle. Not adverse at all, quite normal and I thought about those poor bastards across the Atlantic that had lost everything in that devastating hurricane. That's adverse weather but no, some chinless wonder over here rushing about in a hurry because they got up late, with incorrect footwear might slip over in a London tube station and without an adverse weather announcement then London Underground will be liable. Sorry but I don't get it. You must have been outside to notice the weather on your way in to the station.

Rant over, I filled out the necessary return to work paperwork, told them what medication I was on, put on my glasses and went downstairs and was given my first job, to help tidy up before the bosses had their evening walk round inspection. I was given the wine aisle to dress, bringing the glass bottles forward to make the shelves look full and tidy, probably the worst aisle to give someone with double vision but I didn't care. My team leader gave me an internal store phone to look after while he quickly went to the toilet so I began to tidy up. I had to feel my way along the shelf front as my vision meant all the bottles overlapped and the store lights were reflecting off the glass at all angles. I had no idea what I was looking at or if I was doing a good job or not but no one complained so I carried on, then the phone rang, I thought this is a chance to get back in the swing of things, so I answered it. Perfect timing. A clear, well spoken voice on the other end told me their name and that they were ringing in sick for their shift tonight. They told me they had a slight cough and didn't want to come in and start coughing over people. Ah bless, and I felt my temperature start to rise very quickly and I must admit I'd stopped listening and for a few seconds I lost it. All I've been through, I can't see properly, I've got hardly any balance and you're telling me you're not coming in because you've got a slight cough. I just said 'Tough, get your fucking arse in here now!' and down went the phone, or something like that, I think I elaborated a bit more. I never did find out who that was or if they came in that night and to tell you the truth, I don't really want to. Definitely not the sort of person you want next to you in the trenches. I did feel guilty afterwards when I calmed down. Who the hell am I to decide if you feel ill or not? The last type of person I want to be is the person who's got everything worse than you, we all know someone like that, right?

A lot of staff were coming up to me, hugging me and welcoming me back which felt great, I'd worked with some of these people for a long time. It was lovely to hear and feel genuine warmth and sympathy from not just my work colleagues, but my friends. There was one that did disappoint me when they asked me straight away if I was going to sue the company? Eh, are you serious? What for? This bastard, who I don't think had ever said hello to me before, wasn't interested in my welfare, only if I was going to take on the establishment. I just replied 'I'm much better thank you, now Fuck Off!' Then the God squad came to say hello, a couple of lovely ladies who are practicing Christians in every way and good luck to them. Now you can probably tell I'm not at all religious. I don't believe in God but I have no problem with those who do, whatever your faith, whoever you believe in. It provides billions of people worldwide with strength and comfort and gives us law and order and I'll always respect that, but when I heard 'God saved you' it did annoy me. No, the expert medical teams saved me, science and medicine saved me, don't belittle their work and effort otherwise get rid of the NHS now and let God take over. If God did save me then surely by definition he would have given me the stroke in the first place. If he did then that is one sick sense of humour. One colleague did give me a hug in front of a customer who then asked me why I had been shown such emotion. I explained this was my first day back since recovering from a stroke and he invited me to speak at his church. 'God has saved you for a purpose' he declared. I politely declined as to speak at church would have been very hypocritical of me. You believe whatever you want to believe in, I respect that, but at the end of the day the Bible was written and translated by people who still thought the world was flat. That's your big clue for me. I'm a lot more open minded than that and I'd have to see hard proof of a superior being.

I worked on tidying bottles of wine, normally a really easy task, but after two hours I was absolutely exhausted. It's one thing going for long walks and sitting at home thinking you're ok. It's something completely different thinking, concentrating and having to do something properly for somebody else. I was extremely conscious about two things. Firstly I found myself hesitating big time when getting asked questions by customers. It took me that little bit longer to take in the info and to think of the correct answer. I found myself trying to disguise long pauses with plenty of involuntarily ums and argh's. I started off being a bit embarrassed but then thought to myself, 'Hey, you've just come back after a stroke. Do they expect you to do a fucking cartwheel after every question' I told myself I was an example to all who had gone through a serious illness and a lot more fortunate than some. This is why I'm back at work, to get better and stronger. Secondly I was worried about my right eye. It was really starting to ache as for the first time in a while it was having to perform normal routines but it was a good ache as I knew it would strengthen with time. It was about 6 o'clock and I was knackered. I'd already been told to go and have a rest at any time but I thought no. That's a very easy routine to get into. If I go for a break today at 6 o'clock, then tomorrow I'll be looking at the time waiting for 6 o'clock. If I want to get better, then I'm sensibly going to have to work through it, so I carried on to the end of my shift. I felt exhausted but proud I was back in some small form. You have to push yourself if you want to recover, don't settle for easy or the nice to do but you also have to listen to your body and know and respect your ever changing limits. The best quote I ever saw was from Arnold Schwarzenegger before he became a film star. He said 'No one has ever climbed a ladder with their hands in their pockets.' Fantastic, apply that to whatever you want.

My job for the first couple of weeks was date checking on the long life tins and packets. The hand held terminal tells you where to go and what items to check so it gets you around the store which was good exercise and good for my memory. This was however harder than I thought, made more difficult by the fact that I couldn't move my eyes quick enough or take in information quickly so it was easy for me to become disorientated in a place I knew so well. I walked through the middle of the shop like I'd done a million times before, looking down each aisle, but I couldn't work out what I had just seen or who I had just seen. Trying to read the dates on the packets did hurt my eyes a bit to start with but like I said before it was a good hurt as I felt they were being exercised. Oh well, I thought. Give it a bit of time.

One aisle I couldn't go down was the carrot aisle. It filled me with horror. The first time I went near it my legs went to jelly and that feeling and the dog whistle noise came flooding back. It was as if my body remembered. I didn't go anywhere near that aisle until I had to be trained on the new online order shopping system which had again been adjusted to try and make it quicker. I had to do a pretend shop with the new handset and the bastard thing sent me straight to the loose carrots. I had to read it three times to make sure I wasn't seeing things. Well it's got to happen sooner or later I told myself and for the first time since that night, I headed up the aisle to the carrots. I tried to hide behind a big, fake smile, always game but inside I was screaming and I thought I was going to pass out. My legs were like jelly, all the memories came flooding back and I found myself holding and staring at the racking in the same place I had done nearly six months ago. It felt like I was wearing a layer of frost but I had done it and I got out of the aisle as quickly as I could. It was the best thing I could have done, although to this day I do not walk down that aisle, unless I'm helping the online order team and I'm directed down that aisle by the handset.

I have been asked a few times by colleagues if I want to return to a more senior position like I had before. Not by the bosses I hasten to add. My answer is a very quick no, I don't even have to think about it and it's for two reasons. Firstly I'm not physically capable anymore, I can't think quick enough and I feel I'm getting older and slower and it wouldn't be fair to anyone on both sides. You have to accept your limits as I've mentioned before, which may change later, or may not. Secondly and this is the more important one, I do not want the silent killer, namely the stress. I'm very happy in the job I'm doing now, I get there early, do what I'm told, work hard, go home, switch off. It worries me when people say at interviews or in off the cuff conversations or on the telly 'Yes I'm good at handling stress!' We've all done it. How do you know? Truth is that's your brain thinking you can but your body just says no and will shut you down without warning when it reaches the level. What's the level? Who knows? Everyone is different. As you go through life, you get more responsibility, a better job, a house, family, kids and more and bits of stress are bolted on with them all like building a wall of lego. It's normally a gradual build up so you don't notice or feel it but it's like the donkey in that game Buckeroo. Trust me, sometimes you don't know what stress is until they take it away from you.

After a month back at work part time I felt ready for the next step. I remembered Mr Schwarzenegger's quote and I felt I could handle it so decided to request to go back full time as a general assistant which they let me do. I was allowed to start at 10am so my body would wake up naturally and I was given a full lunch hour in the middle of my shift. I wasn't exactly being wrapped in cotton wool which I didn't want but I was being looked after in terms of duties and hours worked and I knew I was improving.

CHAPTER EIGHT

Enter The Magician

I first met the magician at my first check up on my second morning in hospital. I had finished being examined by one of his staff who told me straight away 18 months recovery which took a while to sink in. In two minutes he was virtually spot on. Always trust the experts! I remember being pushed in a wheelchair into an area with many computer terminals and specialists to meet the magician. I could barely see but I knew this was a large Asian man of some seniority with a big, long beard. He explained to me how my recovery might go and I listened, confused and disorientated, trying to take it in, right up to the point where he mentioned surgery. That statement sunk in really quickly and I immediately thought no fucking way. I had a difference of fourteen, whatever that means and I was sure that would get better without surgery, the thought horrified me. You can operate on me wherever you need to but as a general rule of thumb I have always told myself I'm never having any surgery on my eyes, my teeth or my bollocks! Anyway, there was no pressure, it was entirely my call so at this point I politely declined.

That was then but now, over fourteen months later, it was clear I needed extra help to get rid of this bastard double/ chameleon vision. It hadn't healed naturally and again I found myself in the position I never wanted to be in, getting used to it rather than getting better. I had given my body the time to heal but the difference had just been too big from the start. I was told originally the difference was 14, however they measure it?? That apparently is huge but I was then told at a later check up it was well over 20 so natural recovery would have been virtually impossible. Looking back I think the magician knew that when he first saw me but fair play he gave me a chance. Your brain always trys to revert to what it thinks is normal. Mine was trying but just couldn't close the difference, it was too great.

So I was now at the point where I needed extra help, I had to face up to it, it wasn't going to heal itself and I was sick of it, enter the magician. I spoke to him at length about what surgery would involve and to be honest I didn't relish it. It involved taking out my right eye, cutting the eye muscles and restitching the muscles tighter into my eyeball and this would get my eyes straight together and hopefully my brain would then synchronise them back as a pair. The other option was to put a stitch through the white of my eye and drag it until it was straight, then stitch it up for the same result. The magician told me he would get my eyes straight, but hang on I thought, surely I'll be the only one who can tell that as I'm the one looking through them and hopefully, I'll be knocked out. The magician told me my eyes would be on adjustable stitches that could be moved like a ratchet after the op. Like I said, I didn't relish it, who would? But the only point that really horrified me were two words, local anesthetic. No I want it done under a general I said. The magician explained that I wouldn't feel a thing but I explained that I would see it and hear it! I don't want to see or hear anything. I wanted it done under a general, knock me out and you can do what you want and thankfully the magician agreed. Now the last thing a medical team want to do to a stroke survivor is put them to sleep so I now had to undergo a number of tests to prove I could handle it. This was something I was not going to fail. I'm being very careful in this book to call myself a stroke survivor and not a stroke victim!

I had a number of tests over the next few weeks, blood, weight, others and I made sure I told the truth so the results were accurate. I wanted this op but it now everything felt very serious. If I was bluffing or bullshitting I was dead on the table or at least severely fucked up so the act I had put on for the kids and for work disappeared. It was no longer perception deception. If I played ball and did what I was told, then the magician would fix me. The medical team would have known I was bluffing anyway. On October 20th, after my last set of tests, I got the nod to get knocked out. My op was going to happen on the 25th November, nearly sixteen months after my stroke. I was overjoyed and I started counting down the days. This felt like the last part of my recovery, a huge milestone and hopefully the final piece of the jigsaw.

I always try to use the term milestone rather than target. Always acknowledge milestones rather than set targets in any recovery. When your baby is born, you don't set it a target to walk in six months but you are overjoyed when you see them reach this major milestone. It's the same recovering from any serious illness. We are all different and heal at different speeds so don't put extra pressure on yourself and feel possible stress and dejection by failing to hit a target. Just celebrate milestones, improvements, turning points and key moments, no matter how slight or minor other people may see them as. To you they are huge and important.

Bollocks, I had a ticket for Simple Minds the same day as my op, my favourite group from the eighties. I'd waited nearly thirty years to go and see them play live. Typical, but in the end not a hard choice to make, I wanted to see properly again more than anything. The night before the op I was very jittery. I just wanted it over but it felt like time was dragging then stopping. I compiled a selection of my favourite tunes on a playlist on my laptop so I could just lie there in the darkness after my op with my headphones on and relax. I was aware there was a one in four chance this op wouldn't work but as you can probably tell by the references to horse racing in this book and those who know me anyway know I like the odd weekly gamble and I'll back a 3-1 winner any day of the week and twice on Sundays. The magician had told me I still might have double vision on both peripherals but ahead would be fine. That would be a million times better than what I had now. This was going to fucking hurt. It was going to look and feel like I'd been hit by a bus and the stitches were going to rub like bitches in my eye sockets for a couple of weeks but that was nothing compared to the elation I was going to feel when I could see properly again, my family, my friends, what I'm eating, where I'm having a piss, etc.

It was a typical cold, miserable November morning the next day, but to me it was beautiful. I got up and out nice and early and walked up to the hospital by myself, completely relaxed in my own little world. Surgery started at 7.30, the magician was doing the op himself and I wanted to make sure I was one of the first to go in. I remember thinking to myself on the way up 'This is nearly over mate' and I kept thinking of how I would be in a couple of weeks time when I had healed and my stitches had dissolved. I found my check in ward, did the paperwork and sat in the waiting area in silence with a few nervous looking others.

I didn't have to wait long, only a few minutes and I was led into a small private room where I was told to get changed. I got dressed into your standard back to front, arse out hospital gown and long, white elastic socks. At least they kept part of me warm. I was then called and I walked down the hospital corridor and through two big double doors into a sort of waiting area. Result, I must be first. There were two big Aussie doctors in the room talking about rugby and they told me to lie down. They were so casual and at no point did I hear the term needle, injection or any of the usual phrases to get your heart up a notch. They just put me to sleep.

I came round later in the same room, eager to see what my new world looked like but aware I had a dressing covering my right eye that I dare not touch. After a few minutes and a couple of tests I was wheeled back to a little private room where my other half was waiting. Shortly after, the magician came in with one of his staff to have a check on his work. I sat up as he removed my dressing and the first thing I looked at was my other half. She looked perfect, single vision and it was an amazing feeling. I very nearly cried but I didn't want to ruin my surgery. I then looked across at the magician. I saw him perfectly and I think it's time you know who he is. The magician is Dr Ali, Leading eye specialist not just in Moorfields, St George's but all over the world. He is known and respected everywhere and experts and students from all parts of Britain come to him to learn and train. The work he does is truly magic and I'm sure many of his patients feel the same way.

Anyway he hadn't finished with me yet. He wanted to make sure his work was perfect and so did I. By now my Dad had joined the room and Dr Ali took a small penlight out of his pocket and told me follow it across the room and tell him when it became two lights. As my eye rolled to the left I felt it bump and roll over my stitches. It didn't hurt, maybe I was in euphoria at seeing properly again or maybe I was dosed up on painkillers, didn't matter. The light split into two as it moved, resembling a double helix, so my stitches had to be adjusted. This is the part that still makes my teeth itch.

I lay completely still looking up, while my eye was clamped wide open, just like that scene out of Clockwork Orange. Two large metal needle things were then put under my eyelids to grab the adjustable stitches and the light was shone again up to my left. This was horrible, I felt these pieces of metal under my eyelids and on my eye lashes but I told myself to relax. It was impossible to look away and I had two fistfuls of bedclothes that I was close to tearing. I was asked if I was ok, I just gritted my teeth and replied calmly 'Fine Thanks', yet every bone in my body was screaming 'For Fuck's Sake Hurry Up!'. I felt my eye being pulled across, jumping on a ratchet by Dr Ali's assistant until the two lights became one and he tied the stitches, put the dressing back and told me to rest, it was over. Dr Ali told me under no circumstances was I to touch my eye, even with the dressing, that would pop the stitches and ruin his magic. As soon as he said that I wanted to rub it, typical. Also under no circumstances was I to go swimming for the next month. Oh no, my Speedo's will have to remain in the drawer. No problem, I haven't been swimming for about twenty years and have no desire to start now. Another doctor came in and asked if I wanted a sandwich. Yes I do, in my excitement I'd completely forgotten I'd been fasting because of my op and hadn't eaten since yesterday lunchtime, I was bloody famished. He brought me a tuna sandwich and it didn't touch the sides. I damn well nearly ate my fingers as well. I now couldn't wait to go home and do nothing but listen to a bit of music.

I felt a bit hazy as I left the hospital, a big white dressing covering my right eye and my Dad gave me a lift home. I crawled into bed and went to sleep, all the pent up excitement and adrenalin had taken its toll.

Fucking Hell, I woke up later that evening in an absolute world of pain. Whatever drugs I'd been given for my op had clearly worn off and my head felt as if it was on fire with a lava filled eye socket. I could also feel my stitches, like a ring of needles, around the back of my eye so I tried not to move them. Try closing your eyes and keeping them still, it's virtually impossible. I'd been given a load of painkillers to take every few hours but again I decided not to take them. I didn't want to be dependent on them like last time so I just went for the eye drops I'd also been given. I pulled back my dressing and squirted them in. These were lovely and cool and provided a small bit of relief for a few seconds but the fire quickly returned. I told myself not to worry about now but to think about two weeks time and just relax and try and go back to sleep, fuck listening to music. I knew what I had just gone through was the best decision I had ever made.

After a couple of days of agony, I started to adjust and I wanted to have a look at my new world. I lay on my bed, pulled off my dressing and threw it away and I was in awe with what I saw. I saw the door frame and the light fitting, the butterfly and the dinosaur absolutely crystal clear and just the one of them. The hours I had spent over the previous sixteen months trying to achieve the vision I was now looking at totally overwhelmed me. I then looked left, my stitches scraping and prodding at my eye's soft tissues but I didn't feel pain. Instead I just stared at the butterfly and dinosaur on the bedroom wall and for the first time I saw how beautiful and colourful they really were. I had about 85% perfect vision. Straight ahead and left was fine but my peripheral on my right was just a mess of different colours. But this was superb, amazing and now I wanted more. I was eager to see my new world and decided to take a walk down the shops. I got dressed, put on a pair of clear glasses for protection and had a look at myself in the mirror. I thought a terminator was looking back at me, my right eye was totally red where it had filled with blood but I could see myself perfectly. I got out the door but after about twenty yards I realized what a bad idea this was. You don't realize how much your eyes move naturally. It was quite windy and everytime something moved or made a noise my eyes were immediately drawn to it. This really hurt, my stitches felt like they were shredding and slicing my eyes with the movement. I went another twenty feet and gave up. 'No way, this is far too soon' I thought and I turned round and went back to the safety of my bedroom. I had been signed off work for a couple of weeks for a reason. Always listen to the experts! The next few days did go pretty quickly and again I felt myself eager to get back to work. I was starting to feel a completely different person and I needed to get back to my responsibilities.

CHAPTER NINE

Giving Something Back

I was at work one day around November, about a year later from my eye op, upstairs in the canteen having my lunch, reading one of the free local papers that always seem to litter the place, when an article caught my attention. It was for the Stroke Association and I shut myself off from the outside world and read it intently. It gave me inspiration reading about the work I already knew that they tirelessly achieve and gave me an idea for a chance to give something back. I had known for a while that I wanted to do something, some way of putting back into a system I had taken so much out of and owe more than I would ever be able to repay. I also wanted to do something physical that would lay a lot of my ghosts to rest, something that could push my physical limits up another couple of notches which would in turn help the continued building of my confidence. Let's go straight to Google.

I closed the paper and pulled out my phone, went straight to Google and searched for fundraising events for the Stroke Association.

I was amazed to see how many events there was to choose from all over the country so I looked for one around the London area and Bingo. I saw a 'Resolution Run' in Hyde Park coming up in March in a few months. This would be just under three years since I had my stroke. Perfect I thought, nice and local plus that will give me a chance to get some sponsorship money. I had the option of a 5km run or a 10km run. I went for the 10km option as this would test me further and help me achieve knocking some ghosts out. I paid out the entrance fee on my phone and signed up immediately. Then I waited patiently for a couple of days for my entry pack to come through the post.

Sure enough it came a couple of days later, a sponsorship form, a newsletter and other paperwork, the iconic purple Stroke Association top which I was going to run in and my running number which I had to fix to my top. On the back of my number were some emergency details I had to fill out in case something went wrong, like what? This made me think. I can't see properly out of my right side, I get seriously disorientated, have little balance, suffer fatigue at strange times, I'm overweight, out of condition and both my knees are fucked. I'm running on behalf of the Stroke Association and now I'm worried about having a heart attack. 'Hang on, slow down, relax!' I told myself. You're one of the fortunate ones. Think of those that you're doing this for, the medical experts plus carers and families that look after those who weren't so damn lucky as I was. I knew from that moment I would not fail to finish this run. It was not a race, it was about achieving something physically challenging whilst giving something back.

I waited for November to pass as I didn't want to take anything away from the poppy appeal, then December I set up a Justgiving page linked to my facebook page and started sharing it about, updating it every week to keep it fresh. I wanted to raise at least £500, a tiny amount for the cause but I thought this would be achievable as we had just over five hundred colleagues at work so if a big percentage of them put in then I'll be able to make the balance through friends and family, but surely there was more I could do? We still had some official Stroke Association collecting shaker pots at work so I asked if I could use them and put up some sort of poster about my run on the sales floor. The bosses agreed and I put a cheesy little A4 poster of myself and a brief little bit of narrative on what I was doing and why and I put it with a shaker pot on one of our service desks at the back of the store that I frequently served on. I was astonished at the amount of people who gave their change who had been affected by stroke in their family. It seemed as if everyone I served had a family member or friend that was in their own struggle with stroke and a lot of people shook my hand and wished me luck.

One regret I had was that we never got to set up the face painting that myself and another colleague had tried to organize. This colleague used to do proper face painting at shows and fairs, so it would have been a proper event and we were both prepared to come in on a couple of Sundays on our day off and do face painting for the kids, with all money taken going in the pot. We had to cancel at the last minute because no one could agree on liability if anything went wrong or in other words, who do we blame? Like what for fucks sake? We know what we're doing. Perhaps a child would slip off the stool and cry, emergency! Or perhaps a parent wouldn't know that their little angel might suffer an allergic reaction to non allergic paints, ludicrous! For fucks sake, when I was a kid we'd come home from playing in the park, always before the street lights came on, covered in shit, bruised and clothes either covered in mud or cut to shreds. We got cleaned up, usually with a clip round the ear for getting our clothes dirty and the next day we went out, in some cases sent out to do the same all over again. We learnt things, built things, interacted with others, used our imagination and made the rules of the playground. Nowadays it's all Playstation, Big Macs and cotton wool. I'm waiting for technology to create a machine that wipes your arse, such is the society we have created.

Sorry rant over. I had to find some kit to run in, I couldn't just run in my purple top and a pair of boxer shorts, that would be scary. No, I knew exactly what I wanted and where to get them. I wanted a pair of white Arsenal shorts, the club has been a massive part of my life for over forty years so I wanted to run around with their badge on me. I needed something familiar, something that was me. I also bought of pair of their yellow socks. I figured if there was a big crowd then I would stand out and be easily recognized in yellow socks. Don't ask me why?? Purple, white and yellow, I thought that was a cracking, stand out from the crowd combination.

It was a lovely, sunny Sunday morning on the day of the run. I had done absolutely no training, certainly hadn't watched my diet but I did have a good night's sleep. I didn't see why I should be training. Like I said before it wasn't a race and I'm sure even with my problems I'll still be in a lot better shape than some of the people I was hoping to run with. I wanted to do this as a normal person and see what I could achieve, it had to be as natural as possible. If I trained it would almost feel like I was cheating, it wouldn't be accurate and I would always have that doubt that I had prepared for it. No I was going in cold and raw, it was the only way I could be sure if I could handle it. I got to Hyde Park by tube, found the big checking in area and attached one of their metal tags to my shoe. I'm not sure if this was a timing device or a location warning device, if it didn't move for a long time then hopefully they would send out a search party. I sat down and waited for the off with that exited feeling you get before a big game.

I looked around and there was already quite a crowd, a sea of purple, a few hundred limbering up, clearly with all different stories to tell. There were a few that had the sign 'Stroke Survivor' hand written on their tops. They all looked really fit and well, one girl in particular I remember who was doing a warm up and looked fit as a fiddle and this gave me a huge boost. Others were huddled in pairs or groups with photos of what were clearly friends and family who had passed from stroke attached to their tops. There must have been a load of money raised by our group, everyone had their own story of why they were there and it was a very powerful feeling.

During the weeks before the event I did have a couple of people offering to do the run with me which would have been lovely. I'd said yes because how could I deny anyone running for the charity and they would have been good company. But they had pulled out and honestly I was more than glad I was doing this by myself. I wanted to be on my own, push myself, motivate myself and challenge myself. I didn't want anyone pushing or pulling me along. Now I knew I wasn't going to run the full 10km, those days are long gone. They were never there to begin with but I made up my mind to run the first kilometer and then push myself to run as much of the rest as I could. I owed that to the people that had kindly and generously sponsored me and I wasn't just going to walk it. We did a bit of a warm up as a group led by one of the huge number of volunteers and then made our way to the start line. I made myself comfortable near the back of this huge purple crowd and a big cheer went up as the ribbon went up and the purple crowd headed up the course. As far as I was concerned, I could have been running in the Olympics and I wanted to help the people I was running for.

I started with a light jog and soon most people were either in the distance or behind me. I was in a nice little bit of space by myself which was perfect. I kept going at my own speed in my own world and then saw the 1km sign, I thought it had come up pretty quickly. Every km is signposted so you know what you're doing. I passed this first sign and started walking, I had achieved the first milestone and I didn't feel too bad but was glad of the rest. For the first five kilometers it was a mixture of light jogging and quick walking. My feet on the concrete were creating a cracking bassline in my head so I added the rest of the tune mentally, including the essential high hat and started breathing to it so managed to switch off for long periods, keeping the rhythm going like a racehorse, but my limited energy was clearly draining out of me. There was a huge fella about 20 yards in front of me, a young lad plodding along like me, clearly pushing himself like I was, so I decided to use him as my pacemaker. I ran ahead of him and every time I heard his heavy footsteps get closer behind me, I ran on a bit further and played a great bit of cat and mouse. Thinking about it now, he may have been using me as a pacemaker and was trying to catch me up. Whatever it was it was working for both of us. This lad got ahead of me just before the 5km mark, which was back at the start, and he stopped. He had completed his 5km run, my number told the organisers I was doing the 10km run and I was sent on to do another lap. This had now become a bit easier as on this lap I now knew where the km signs were so I could pace myself better and sort the bits I was going to walk. On the first lap I had kept asking myself 'Where the fuck are these signs?'

On the second lap I said Thank You to all the volunteers that I passed who were marshalling the course, clearly in their own time. I also made a point of running past them instead of walking. No I wasn't trying to impress but just a way of showing my gratitude for their support and time for the event, they had made the effort so I was showing them I was too. I was mixing plodding with walking and getting round just fine. I was completely on my own as everyone had strung out, most I think had done the 5km option. I knew I was near the back somewhere but I knew I wasn't last either and there was no way I wasn't going to finish. I was really enjoying it, the sun was still out and I was full of a sense of achievement. The only downside was the amount of people in the park, clearly local chinless wonders, who thought this was their park and were out for a Sunday stroll. They were walking five and six abreast across the paths we were trying to run down and didn't move, not even when a hoard of purple was coming towards them. They did that thing that you see a lot of on the tube and on pavements where they pretend not to see you and look in every other direction but straight at you. Ignorant bastards!

After the 8km sign I felt a huge twinge in my left achilles. 'Oh fuck no' I thought, not this close to home. I snapped my right achilles about fifteen years ago thinking I could still play football and that was twelve weeks in plaster. Still, I've been through a lot worse and I carried on, even managing to run the last five hundred metres or so at speed and finished to a few cheers from the volunteers that were still doing such a fine job. I finished in one hour and twenty five minutes, hardly a world record but as I crossed the finishing line I realized I could push myself a little bit more from now on. I don't need to be worried when doing something physical. I don't have to be worried about feeling that head rush or hearing that dog whistle just because I'm out of breath or I've got up too quick. I had definitely put a couple of ghosts to bed and added a few more levels to my confidence. I could barely move the next day, damn I ached. I ached in places I never knew I had and I was walking as if someone had shoved a broomstick up my arse. Importantly though it was ache and stiffness with a fair bit of pride, not hurt or pain or regret. Fuck me though was I glad I had booked the day off work! More importantly, I checked my Justgiving page and together with the money raised at work, the total was sitting at just over £1.6k. I was gobsmacked, sincerely amazed and humbled at not only people's generosity but at the huge numbers of my friends that stroke had affected. It was so much more than I'd hoped for and it made it so worthwhile. I sincerely thank all those who supported and sponsored me.

CHAPTER TEN

Onwards and Upwards

So how am I now, three and a half years on? I'm still working full time in the same place as a general assistant and I'm so grateful they kept faith in me. I've worked on a couple of different departments that I hadn't before so I've been learning new things from different people. The bosses have changed a couple of times but the mutual respect hasn't, I have always felt that I have been treated brilliantly by bosses who could put on the company head without taking off the personal head at the same time. They let me ease back in and helped to build up my confidence and my strength at my pace but of course with encouragement. This took so much weight off my shoulders as you have so many doubts as you recover as to what role you think you'll be able to return to eventually, as a colleague, as a friend, as a family member, as a father and as a man. I'll always be grateful for that. I'm a general assistant, not exactly the end of the rainbow stuff but part of a team with a role to play and it's a good role that fits in with what I wanted to achieve physically and mentally. I remember my first day back, hardly able to see or keep balance and being exhausted after a couple of hours and I realise how far I've come. I arrive at work, do what I'm told to do, work hard then go home and switch off. The one thing I don't do is play host to the silent killer! I don't wake up in the middle of the night wondering who's in first thing or if I've forgotten something for the boss, have I done this, have I done that? I don't have that stress anymore. That was the biggest thing I have tried to reduce, not just at work but in my life as a whole which must have been a massive factor for me to have a stroke in the first place. I work hard but sensibly, working sensible hours. Gone are the long shifts with a quick bite to eat somewhere in the middle and I no longer work any night shifts. I've never volunteered for them since I returned and they wouldn't let me do them anyway. I change the odd shift here and there to help out but generally I work the same hours daily with a proper lunch break, time away to sit down and eat properly and let it go down. More blood is transferred to the digestive system after you eat away from other parts of your body so let your dinner go down. It does scare me sometimes when I see some of the others at times rush in, scoff something down then rush out again. Remember your brain will tell you that this is fine, I can handle it, but your body will shut you down without warning if you cross it's line.

I've slowed the pace of my life down a lot and I'm definitely not afraid to say no to anyone and not just do something to please others. I used to be very much a 'Last minute Lionel' but now if I'm travelling anywhere or going to work, I'll get there nice and early with time to spare for a cup of tea and a sit down. I can't remember the last time I rushed for anything, not even to catch the bookies before closing and there must be a brisk walk to work each week to get the old heart and lungs pumping. It's not far, about thirty minutes tops but that's my exercise for the week.

I still haven't picked up my guitar properly, I just can't get the muscle memory right, yet, but I am going to football matches on my own. I'm not fantastic in big crowds but I can certainly look after myself in that respect. I do go to Arsenal occasionally, that will never leave me but I mainly concentrate on the lower leagues, clubs that still cater for your average fans and not the big clubs that chase the corporate dollar. I had achieved the famous ninety two before my stroke, seeing a game at all ninety two league grounds in England and Wales, It was something that I loved doing, seeing a bit of the country at the same time, so I have kept this up with the new teams promoted to the league and I'm taking it a bit further. I want to reach the milestone of seeing a game at two hundred grounds worldwide, however long it takes me. I have no schedule, just take it as it comes, as I write this, including the ones I visited before my stroke, I'm on over one hundred and forty.

My eyesight has been fine. It's remained at 85% but that is still single vision. Dr Ali, the magician, his work was magnificent and permanent so far. I had an eye test recently as the world was getting a bit blurred and I thought my right eye was starting to turn in again but they are dead plum level. It's just a bit of age creeping up on me so I have now got a proper pair of prescription glasses. I still have my original pair with the left side blanked out, the photo on the cover of this book is the actual pair I used during recovery and then kept for sentiment. They served me well.

Although my double vision is no more when I look straight ahead, my right eye is very lazy. It does take me a split second sometimes for them to come together when I move my head and this affects my ability to take in information quickly, especially if something's coming towards me. This isn't my eyes, just the signal between them and my brain. My stroke completely blew that bridge and the rebuilding has come to a premature end before completion. I used to hate people throwing things at me to catch, a pen, a sweet, keys etc because I just lost sight of them somewhere along their trajectory and guessed where to put my hands to catch them. I either feel them hit my palms or, as in most cases, hear them crash into the floor. It's not as bad as it was but I still can't fix properly on anything that's moving too quick. If you say hello to me as you're walking past, my eyes won't get there in time so I'll have to rely on voice recognition. If I just reply 'Hello mate' then there's a good chance I haven't got a clue who you are, it just hasn't registered and that's the standard reply I've mastered to save embarrassment and percepted ignorance. I often find myself closing my right eye to get a better look at something, especially if I'm looking right. That's my brain naturally trying to help. Neither can I look up. I'm like dog, my eyes just can't do it. Sounds strange but I can't play pool or snooker properly as I can't look from the top of my eyes, I'm not sure how to describe that?? If I'm going upstairs at work or at the station, I can't look up to see who if anybody is coming down and if I do it disorientates me and I get dizzy. Even doing something simple, say looking up at the information boards at the train station can make me feel really wobbly and the same happens if I look right. The 15% I can't see properly on my right periphery is just double vision and a lot of different colours. I used to joke that if you're going to do me then hit me on my right side. I probably won't see it and if I do, then there's probably fuck all I can do to stop it as I hesitate. It is slightly better than it was but that's my brain translating the information better. It used to be this big translucent screen which turned blue, orange and red which was a pain in the arse because I kept jerking my head to get rid of it. It was like looking through a different coloured translucent shower curtain which was kind of funky but that drove me absolutely fucking nuts for months but after a while you get used to it and accept it. Before then it resembled a moving digital read out like the Matrix which was even worse but as I have said many times, I would have taken this at the start.

I still get really dizzy when I look right, again it's the information getting lost in translation. If I find myself looking right quickly, then my brain overrides me, say if I'm crossing the road or at work and I have this feeling like the world is crashing over me from the right like a big wave. It feels real enough put me off balance and you will see me take the odd corrective step when it happens but again this has got slightly better with time. I used to hate it if I was walking in a crowded area because everyone just automatically thinks you're pissed. I went on a boat party with work on the Thames and that really played havoc with my senses. It already felt as if I was on a boat and now I was on a real boat. I spent most of the night rooted to one spot thinking how lucky I was that I don't suffer with sea sickness. It still feels like I'm on a boat most of the time and the world feels like a cross channel ferry at times but my sea legs have got stronger with time.

I'm really conscious that I still hesitate, like the signal between my brain and body is jammed somewhere. I can only describe it as a conversation between my brain and say, my left hand. My left hand for example will say ' Hello brain, I need to pick this cup up, give me a hand.' My brain replies 'Go on then hand, I've got you.' My left hand then says ' Well anytime today will be nice!' and my brain just says 'Fuck off I'm having a tea break!' It doesn't bother me that much and people say they can't tell but I can tell and I really notice it. That's why it's all public transport for me now. I mentioned before I snapped my right achilles tendon a few years ago now and I haven't driven since then. That's your brake foot so driving wasn't the problem, it was stopping. But now, no way, even the thought horrifies me. What if I'm driving along and a kid runs out in front of me and I hesistate. Bang. I'd never be able to live with myself. Also if someone comes up on my right or someone crosses the road from the right then there's a good chance I won't see them, again I don't want to go there. I live in South London, transport links here are fantastic, you can get literally anywhere and work is local so I don't miss the car at all.

I was immediately put on lots of different medication after my stroke, most of which I'm still on today and I always make sure I'm not even close to running out. On top of my medication for asthma, I also take blood thinners and anti chorlesterol tablets. The blood thinners make me bruise easily. I've only got to take a small knock and it looks like I've been horse whipped. I wake up some mornings and I've got bruises in places that I just don't recall getting a knock. I hardly drink at all now, the odd couple on a night out perhaps but it feels like the alcohol is travelling a little bit quicker round my body in thinner blood. I really don't recommend it.

I still get down days, I think that's par for the course but again nothing like the massive extremes I experienced before. There's things I'm just not capable of doing anymore and any further recovery is now extremely unlikely. But always look at where you started from and you have to keep reminding yourself of how far you've come already. This definitely comes with time, the frustrations lessen and learning to accept your new limits is a huge factor. I do still get tired quickly, as if my brain is saying 'That's enough for today mate' and always at weird times, not necessarily after anything physical. That's your body talking to you, I recommend you listen to it.

Where will I be in another six months? Who knows but I know I'll be thinking I'm so much better than I was six months ago. Recovery isn't a race, it's a long, hard marathon with plenty of ups and downs but just keep at your own pace and look forward, not necessarily to a specific time but to something specific physically or mentally you want to do, however simple it may seem to others, it's huge to you. Don't forget to be proud and recognize these milestones.

This has been the worst three and a half years physically for me but without question the best three and a half years educationally. I'd like to think that I was never a nasty person, impatient definitely but never nasty. If we ever agreed to meet at 8pm then be there latest a couple of minutes before or I would get very twitchy. I look at things, life, people in a much different way today. I'm a lot calmer, have more patience with people and my life is definitely 20mph slower and it's starting to line up nicely with my age. The worst trap to fall into is thinking 'Yeah, I can still do that'. I'm a lot more patient as a person now. Patience was never a family trait but now I may be waiting for someone who, unbeknown to anyone, is having their own battle with illness, no problem, I can wait, or better still, help. What a pity it took something so serious to change a basic human trait. I catch myself looking at ambulances speeding past. I'm still working and living just round the corner from St George's so there's plenty to choose from. I wonder who's on board and why? Every ambulance you see has a story and a struggle to deal with and not just for the person in it. I get asked a lot if there's one thing I would change if I went through it again then what would that be? My answer to that is always very quick and simple. Change my lifestyle so I don't have to go through it again!

Thank you for reading my story, love and peace to all xx

Lightning Source UK Ltd.
Milton Keynes UK
UKHW01f1327260918
329553UK00014B/1506/P